REPETITION

The Library of Religion and Culture
General Editor: Benjamin Nelson

HARPER TORCHBOOKS

EDITORS' NOTE: *A check-list of Harper Torchbooks, classified by subjects, is printed at the end of this volume.*

REPETITION

An Essay In Experimental Psychology

SØREN KIERKEGAARD

TRANSLATED
WITH INTRODUCTION AND NOTES
BY WALTER LOWRIE

HARPER TORCHBOOKS *The Cloister Library*
HARPER & ROW, PUBLISHERS
NEW YORK, EVANSTON AND LONDON

Printed in the United States of Amercia.

This book was originally published by Princeton University Press in 1941 and is here reprinted by arrangement. The Torchbook edition omits the Editor's Preface and an essay, 'How Kierkegaard got into English' by Walter Lowrie.

First HARPER TORCHBOOK edition published 1964 by
Harper & Row, Publishers, Incorporated
49 East 33rd Street
New York, N.Y. 10016

CONTENTS

EDITOR'S INTRODUCTION

by Walter Lowrie

INSTEAD of the motto we now read on the back of the title page of *Repetition* S.K. first proposed to write the words of Solomon in Proverbs 5:15, "Drink waters from thine own well." This indeed was a counsel which he followed in all his works, but especially in this book and in the mate to it which was published on the same day, October 16, 1843. For *Fear and Trembling,* though it was ascribed to a different pseudonym, was a companion to this book. Although one is couched in the loftiest style of "dialectical lyric," and the other professes to be "an essay in experimental psychology" and is characterized by one of S.K.'s pseudonyms as a "whimsical" book, both deal symbolically with the problems which the author faced in his greatest crisis, when by the renunciation of marriage with the woman he loved he cut himself off from the only hope of leading a normal human life and was forced to recognize himself as "the exception to the universal human." In *The Point of View* S.K. refers to this moment as the occasion of his decisive conversion. In his pseudonymous works this fact is not so evident, for the reason that the reputed authors, who are conceived of as themselves living in the aesthetic stage, cannot consistently look beyond the field of their experience and see the religious consummation of the struggles which they witness. If they had been able to see beyond "the borders of the marvellous," they might have been able to describe the situation which S.K. in his own name depicts in the Edifying Discourses with which he scrupulously "accompanied" his pseudonymous works. Unfortunately his contemporaries paid no heed to these which were the best of all introductions, and alas, his modern commentators in Germany have almost completely ignored them. How pertinent they are will be seen at the end of this Introduction, where I quote a passage from the third of the *Three Edifying Discourses* which also were published on October 16, 1843, by a different bookseller. The pseudonymous authors, though they could see that Repetition was the same thing as the Platonic Recollection, only with a movement forward instead of backward, and that it might well be substituted for the Hegelian "mediation," were yet unable to see that in the religious sphere it meant subjectively (on man's part) the fruits of repentance, and transcendently (on God's part) atonement!

All of S.K.'s works deal symbolically with his own experience. Professor Hirsch has justly remarked that the tendency to express his experiences symbolically is evident in the earliest entries of the *Journal*, and that this was conjoined with an extraordinary aptitude for viewing them objectively. This observation, if only we stretch it more broadly, goes far to account for the most striking characteristic of S.K.'s literary production, his habit of ascribing his works to pseudonymous authors, some of whom deal in turn with a multiplicity of fictitious characters. A German author, Martin Thust, perversely compared S.K.'s characters to a marionette theater. One is following a false scent when one seeks to explain S.K.'s use of pseudonyms as a deliberate and artful device. In fact this was evidently so spontaneous that it might rather be referred to a compulsion psychosis. Yet the word "theater" is suggestive, for it was S.K.'s dramatic instinct which prompted him to give expression not only to his experiences but also to his possibilities by the use of the actor's mask. His characters may properly be called *persons* in this sense, the sense of the Latin word *persona*. We state the case broadly enough when we affirm that S.K., though he had an extraordinary aptitude for philosophic abstraction and was capable of coining definitions which are abstract to the last degree, was nevertheless strongly inclined by his poetic genius to express every human experience, his own experiences especially, in symbolical terms, that is to say, dramatically, in concrete situations and personifications. I would remark here (anticipating a quotation I shall make later) that this "interest" was the rock upon which S.K.'s metaphysic foundered, or rather it was this tendency to express everything concretely, "existentially," which obscures for us his metaphysics. Furthermore, because S.K.'s own experiences were objectivated in fictitious characters, we do not at once perceive how personal his works are.

When once we know that all his works were waters drawn from his own well, it is evident that we cannot expect to understand them thoroughly without a rather intimate knowledge of his life. But now, when all of S.K.'s works are or are about to be published in English, this very necessary introduction evidently cannot be furnished with each volume. Such knowledge must be assumed on the part of the reader, and anyone can get it from my *Kierkegaard,* especially pp. 191-271, or from briefer biographies. In my opinion, what needs to be done by way of introducing each work is to furnish from the *Papers,* which probably never will be published in English, and from the *Journal,* and from occasional comments in the works, passages in which S.K. (or a pseudonym) elucidates his own thought.

Like *Either/Or,* the two following works (with which we are now dealing) were written "for her," and they contain passages which only Regina could be expected to understand fully—passages, for example, which apparently carry on arguments which had been begun between the lovers. Nevertheless, any reader who picks up this book without having the least knowledge of S.K.'s story will get a great deal out of it, a great deal of poetry, some fun, and perhaps an apprehension that there is something serious in the idea of Repetition. And if one were to read the book with great attention, giving due heed to significant sentences which here and there are interjected, one ought, according to S.K., to be able to make out the prodigious importance of Repetition as a new category.

But evidently his contemporaries in Denmark were quite incapable of detecting any serious meaning in this book—if we may judge from the fact that Professor J. L. Heiberg, who in a book of his called *Urania* (got up as a New Year's gift, with elegant binding and a gilt edge) praised *Repetition* for its "pretty and telling" passages, but really was praising only the irrelevant thoughts which he had put into it. S.K. was disgusted, and in a bitterly polemical passage he says: "They tell of the case of a man who won a great prize in the lottery and went out of his head for joy. So it was with me when I saw some of my thoughts cited by the Rector Magnificus of Literature, by him corrected *et encomio publico ornati.*; when I saw my name inscribed, if not in the book of life, at least in a gilded New Year's gift-book; saw myself mentioned as one who indeed had not quite said something pretty and telling, but at least almost had said it." He remarked that the Professor evidently "had not read further than the 40th page," whereas it was on the 79th page the serious part of the work began, and began with a repetition of the title in order to prompt the reader's attention. The Professor had pronounced the sententious judgment that "repetition has an essentially different significance in the natural and in the spiritual sphere. The author presumably has had the natural category in view, and perhaps without knowing it has stretched the validity of the concept beyond its proper limits." This sentence contained the correction which S.K. so much resented. And with good reason, for, as the reader can see, there is not a word in the book about repetition in nature—the recurrence of the seasons, of day and night, etc., upon which Professor Heiberg laid stress. Moreover, by the "spiritual sphere" Heiberg, like the good Hegelian he was, had in mind such things as the philosophy of history, etc., which one can "contemplate" disinterestedly, whereas S.K. was thinking of the history of the individual, which to the individual must be of absolute *interest.*

S.K. was so deeply annoyed by this misapprehension that he sat down at once and wrote an open letter addressed to Professor Heiberg by the pseudonym Constantine Constantius. This letter was subjected to several careful revisions; then it was given the form of "A Little Plea, by Constantine Constantius, author of *Repetition*"; finally it was in part rewritten as a letter of Constantine to the reader. Nothing of this was published, but it occupies now 55 pages in the *Papers*. It prompted S.K. to start writing a book which he proposed to call "New Year's Gift, by Nicolaus Notabene, published for the benefit of the asylums." That was not carried far; but it led to the book he called *Prefaces*, ascribed to the same Nicolaus as pseudonym, in which he poked a lot of fun at his friend Professor Heiberg.

The polemic addressed to Heiberg is one of the wittiest things S.K. wrote, but it is far too long to quote here. I have already called attention to a few salient points. But fortunately this egregious misunderstanding led him to give in the same document a much needed explanation of his real intent and a justification of the whimsical way in which he had presented a serious subject. From that I do not hesitate to make a long quotation (which in part is also abstruse or at least philosophical), because I am sure that I can write no better introduction, and that no one can write an introduction so authoritative. It is translated from Vol. IV. of the *Papirer*, pp. 280*ff*.

"The *Repetition* is accompanied by a letter to 'the real reader of the book.' From this letter one learns that 'like Clement Alexandrinus I have tried to write in such a way that the heretics could not understand it.'

"The concept Repetition, when it is employed in the sphere of individual freedom, has a history, in the fact that freedom passes through several stages in order to attain itself. (A) Freedom first is defined as pleasure or in pleasure. What it now fears is repetition, because it is as if repetition possessed a magic power to hold freedom captive when once it had contrived to get it under its influence. But in spite of all the inventiveness of pleasure repetition makes its appearance. Then freedom in pleasure falls into despair. The same instant freedom makes its appearance in a higher form. (B) Freedom defined as shrewdness. Freedom is still in a finite relation to its object and is itself only ambiguously defined aesthetically. Repetition is assumed to exist, but it is the task of freedom to see constantly a new side of repetition. This has found expression in the chapter entitled 'The Rotation of Crops' in *Either/Or*—if I may refer to a recent book. 'The Rotation of Crops' was a factor on the aesthetical side of *Either/Or*, hence this also was shown to be unjustifiable. The men who in freedom stand in no higher relation to the idea commonly prink up this standpoint as the highest wisdom. However, since freedom defined as shrewdness is only finitely characterized, repetition must again make its appearance, that is repetition of the trick by which shrewdness wants to delude repetition and make it something else. Then shrewdness falls into despair. (C) Now freedom breaks forth in its highest form, in which it is defined in relation to itself. Here everything is inverted, and the opposite of the first standpoint is in evidence. Now the highest interest of freedom is to bring about repetition, and it fears only lest change might have the power to alter its eternal nature. Here the problem emerges: *Is repetition possible*? Freedom itself is now repetition. In case it should come about that freedom in the individual, related as it is to the environment, might remain, so to speak, lying in the result, so that it cannot withdraw (repeat itself), then all is lost. So then what freedom now fears is not repetition but change, what it wills is not change but repetition. If then this will to repetition is Stoicism, it contradicts itself and therefore ends by annihilating itself—in order in this way to uphold repetition, which is the same as to throw a thing away in order to have it more securely hid. Then when Stoicism has stepped aside there remains only the religious movement as the true expression of repetition, and in its strife it announces itself with the passionate eloquence of the anxious freedom.

"What was treated under (C) was what I desired to expound in *Repetition*—but not in a learned manner, still less in a manner so scientific that every teller in our philosophical bank could say, 'one, two, three,' I desire to describe and illustrate psychologically and aesthetically; in the Greek sense I would let the concept come into being in the individual, in the situation, working its way out through all sorts of misunderstanding. However, these misunderstandings, in order to get leave to join in, must legitimate themselves, either as witty, or as piquant situations, or as nuances of feeling, or as ironic whimsicalities. This I thought I owed to the reader and to myself, to save my soul from lecturing seriously and with the gravity of a beadle about things everybody might be assumed to know. Repetition (C) is constantly duped by (A) and (B). As it sometimes happens in real life that a bartender, for example, strikingly resembles the King or some other world-historical person, and so when one sees the bartender one is deceived, and then smiles at the deception—so in the case of repetition (C) one is deceived by (A) and (B). As when one is in the street and hears the least little part of a flute-player's piece, and then at that moment the rumbling of wagons and the noise of traffic makes it necessary even for the market-woman to cry in a loud voice if Madame who stands beside her is to hear the price of her cabbage, and then again there is quiet for an instant, and again one hears the flute-player—so in the first part of *Repetition*, (C) is heard at intervals and is drowned by the noise of life. As when a man who knows how to hide a profound conception of life in a simple word sits in the drawing-room conversing with people of various sorts who are using the same word, and then sees on a young girl's lips what it is she really would express, and so he says it for her and to her delight, although she knows it is a misunderstanding and half perceives what the experienced man means and lets the word come out although she knows it is a misunderstanding, and then he incidentally introduces a word drawn from his deeper reflection—so does repetition (C) develop itself in the first part through the chatter of the drawing-room. I myself assume the rôle of Stoicism in order to stand a little higher than (A) and (B), so as to indicate *in abstracto* what *in abstracto* cannot be realized; and meanwhile I prepare everything maieutically for the young man, who really is the one who is to discover the repetition (C) which manifests itself clearly in the second part. As the young man himself is an exception in life, so too is repetition (C), which has like him to fight its way through misunderstandings. The young man's problem is, *whether repetition is possible*. It was as a parody of him that I made the journey to Berlin to see whether repetition was possible. The confusion consists in the fact that the most inward problem is here expressed in an outward way, as though repetition, if it were possible, might be found outside the individual, since it is within the individual it must be found, and hence the young man does exactly the opposite, he keeps perfectly still. Accordingly, the consequence of the journey is that I despair of the possibility and then step aside for the young man, who with his religious primitiveness is to discover repetition. So step by step he discovers repetition, being educated by existence. It appears to him in his distress that Job experienced repetition when he received everything double. What really attracted him to Job, however, was the fact that he was in the right. Upon this point now everything turns. Fate had played him a trick in letting him become guilty. If this is the way it stands, he can never more recapture himself. His nature has become split, and so the question is not about the repetition of something outward, but about the repetition of his freedom. He is glad of the thunderstorm, if only it will come, even though his sentence were to be that no repetition is possible. For the thunderstorm must justify him, that is all he requires. Now providence intervenes with a helping hand, it saves him from his entanglement, and then he bursts out with: 'Is there not then a repetition? Did I not receive everything double? Did I not receive myself again, and precisely in such a way that I must feel doubly the significance of it? And in comparison with such a repetition, what is the repetition of earthly goods which for the spirit are indifferent?' In my accompanying letter I say, 'The young man transfigures repetition as his own consciousness raised to the second power.'

"Everything decisively affirmed about repetition is contained in the second part of the book. Everything that is said in the foregoing part is either jest or only relatively true—as is sufficiently illuminated by the fact that I who said this despair of repetition. And on page 90 I say, 'A religious movement I am unable to make, it is contrary to my nature.' I do not, however, for that reason deny the reality of it or deny that one can learn much from the young man. Moreover, I say in the letter that 'in comparison with the young man I am a person of infinitesimal account,' 'every movement I have made was merely for the sake of throwing light upon him,' 'from the very beginning he has been in good hands, though I often had to tease him so that he might reveal himself.'

"Now if one desires to elucidate the fact that repetition in the world of individuality means something different from what it is in nature and in the case of a plain repetition, I do not know how one can do it more clearly. When in defining repetition one characterizes it as 'transcendent,' as 'a religious movement by virtue of the absurd,' 'when one has arrived at the borders of the marvellous,' when I say that 'eternity is the true repetition,' then I think I have expressed myself pretty intelligibly for the real reader of the book, whom I would beg to forgive me—as I almost would beg the book to forgive me inasmuch as I have deformed its individuality by making obvious what it preferred to hide within itself, desiring only to confide it to the real reader as the meaning of the jest, deformed it by making it more important in the eyes of one intruder or another, since it only desired to go on living as insignificantly as possible in the eyes of the mass, but at the same time to save itself by its insignificance from the pompousness of correction."

We owe it to J. L. Heiberg that S.K.'s ultrapolemical nature was aroused to such a pitch that he gives us here a far more adequate comment upon this book than we have in the case of any other, and therefore prescribes a longer introduction, in inverse proportion to the size of the book. It must be confessed, however, that here S.K. has over-simplified the complexity of this book in two respects.

In the first place, he takes no account of the fact that when he was writing this book in Berlin he indulged the ardent wish that he might yet be reunited with Regina. This fact is plainly attested by the entries of that time in the *Journal.* He wrote on May 17, 1843:

"If I had had faith, I should have remained with Regina. . . . I have begun a story entitled 'Guilty?/Not Guilty?'. It naturally will contain things capable of astonishing the world. . . . But I cannot and will not. My relationship to her shall not be poetically volatilized, it has an entirely different reality. She has not become a theater-princess, so if possible she shall become my wife. O Lord God, that indeed was my only wish, and yet I had to renounce it. . . . Faith hopes also for this life—but, mark well, by virtue of the absurd, not by virtue of human wisdom."

This was the repetition he had first of all in mind as he wrote the book, and naturally he lets Constantine express time and again this all too real notion of repetition as a *redintegratio in statum pristinum.* The constancy of his love or of his nature is doubly expressed in the name of the pseudonym, Constantine Constantius, whom first he proposed to call Walter Constantius. The first name he had in mind was Victorinus de bona speranza. For the hope of victory was strong when he dated this book "Berlin. May, 1843." Alas, this date had to be omitted as an anachronism. The Letter to the Reader, which now is dated "Copenhagen. August, 1843," originally bore the date of "July," and that presumably was the season when he learned that Regina was engaged to another. Perhaps it was then he proposed to describe the book on the title page, not simply as An Essay in Experimental

Psychology, but as "A Fruitless Essay" i. e. attempt. And then perhaps it was he added pathetically to the motto on the back of the title page: "but the fruits of the Spirit are love" (Gal. 5:22).

In the second place, he does not remark upon the new complication which was introduced when he returned to Copenhagen and learned that Regina already was engaged to another. Although this was the solution he ostensibly had been trying to bring about, he was made angry by his unexpected success. It was a matter of course that the book must be altered to meet the changed situation. The statement that the young man in the torment of love "shot himself" was simply erased, and instead of being "dead" he was said to have "disappeared." But at least ten pages had to be torn out after the young man's letter of February 17, and the remainder of the book was completely new. Unfortunately his petulance prompted him to interject phrases here and there, even long passages, expressing profound contempt for a girl who could behave so lightly. We must remember that he fell into exceeding great despair when he learned that "all his sentiments were bosh." This was the moment when he sank to the deepest depths. Fortunately he had the grace to omit most of these passages from the printed book.

This of course added to the complication of the book. This, moreover, was the only work which he did not rewrite, once or even twice, before committing it to the printer. We can well imagine that he was impatient of spending more labor upon a book which already had failed of its purpose.

The passage which I characterized as more "philosophical" is found further along in the same document I have been quoting. It may not be instructive to all, but it surely will seem valuable to some; and inasmuch as it illuminates several of the most characteristic features of S.K.'s thought, it would be a shame if it were not made available in English. It is my hope that the English edition of S.K.'s works will ultimately supply all the prime material necessary for students, whether it is taken from the *Journal* or from other sources. Already, Mr. Dru, in the selections which he has published in *The Journals,* provides for this more fully than the Germans have done in spite of the prodigious literature they have produced on this subject. We are accustomed to concede with a certain awe that the German scholars are *grundlich,* and yet very few of them have taken the pains to learn Danish; and without that knowledge, and the possibility this implies of acquaintance with the sources, it is hardly strange that very few of them in dealing with S.K. have reached conclusions which are deserving of any respect. Schrempf, who is responsible for most of the translations, felt compelled to confess in the face of criticism that his rendering of the original is rather a personal interpretation than a translation and therefore is not so faithful that it can properly serve as the basis for serious study. So he counsels students to put themselves to "not very great trouble" by learning Danish. This he says in his *Nachwort* to the *Abschliesende Nachschrift.*

The passage I am about to quote is not only philosophical but metaphysical. As such it deserves serious attention as an explanation not of this book only but of the works as a whole. For in no other place does S.K. state so clearly his metaphysical position. But first I quote a passage from Constantine's unpublished letter to the reader. It is a brief résumé of what already has been quoted, but it contains one thing more, to which in a metaphysical interest I would direct especial attention. (IV B 120, pp. 308*ff*.).

"That repetition is not merely for contemplation, but that it is the task of freedom, that it signifies freedom itself, consciousness raised to the second power, that it is the *interest* of metaphysics, and at the same time the interest upon which metaphysics founders, that it is the solution of every ethical apprehension, the *Conditio sine qua non* for every dogmatic problem, that the true repetition is eternity—whereas so soon as the problem is stated dogmatically (by following it so far psychologically that it disappears before the eyes of psychology as a transcendency, as a religious movement by virtue of the absurd, which comes to pass when it has reached the borders of the marvellous) repetition will have the meaning of atonement, which no more can be defined by mediation fetched from immanence than can a religious movement which after all is dialectical only in the direction of fate and providence—all this, my dear reader, and everything of the sort, is a misunderstanding which could occur only to one who is unacquainted with the exposition of repetition which we owe to Professor Heiberg and which is as profound as it is original."

Here S.K. refers to a passage in the first part of the book which even a serious reader might stumble over, if he did not overlook it: "Repetition is the *interest* of metaphysics and at the same time the interest upon which metaphysics founders." S.K. rarely makes his metaphysical position clear, for the reason that his "interest in reality" or "the interest of the individual" constantly distracts him from pursuing a metaphysic which is "disinterested," and therefore he says that "metaphysics founders" upon the very thing which prompts one to engage in it, upon the subjective, personal interest which in his case constantly intruded upon the disinterested contemplation of philosophical problems and recalled him to an interest in "existence." For this reason he writes as a psychologist—in this book professedly, in others implicitly.

But now for the metaphysical passage, which attaches itself to the first sentence in this book.

"The Professor accounted for my error by referring to the fact that in my eulogy of repetition what I really had in mind were the categories of nature, and that such was the case seems, as he says, 'to be evident from the fact that he associated repetition with a concept of natural philosophy, viz. *motion*.' When it is established, as the Professor himself teaches, that repetition belongs in the sphere of spirit as well as in that of nature, 'although in the former it has a somewhat different significance,' it follows *eo ipso* that motion also belongs in the sphere of spirit. In our days they have even gone so far as to want to have motion introduced into logic. There they have called repetition 'mediation.' Motion, however, is a concept which logic cannot endure. Hence mediation must be understood in relation to immanence. Thus understood, mediation cannot be employed at all in the sphere of freedom, where the next thing constantly emerges, not by virtue of immanence but of transcendence. The word mediation has therefore occasioned misunderstanding in logic because it permitted the notion of motion to be associated with logic. In the sphere of freedom again the word mediation has been harmful for the fact that, being transferred from logic, it contributed to make the transcendency of motion illusory. To prevent this questionable consequence, or this ambiguous agreement between logic and freedom, I thought that in the sphere of freedom one might use repetition. That it assumes motion is quite true, and substantially this is admitted by Professor Heiberg. . . . Now motion is dialectical not only with respect to space (in which sense it engaged the attention of Heraclitus and the Eleatic School, and later was so much used and abused by the sceptics), but it is dialectical also with respect to time, for the point and the instant correspond to one another. Since I cannot mention two schools by which the dialectic of motion with respect to time is so clearly expressed as Heraclitus and the Eleatics expressed it with respect to space, I therefore mentioned them. Thereby I also gained the advantage that a comic light was shed upon the journey I made to Berlin, be cause 'motion' thereby became a play on words. All such traits are permissible in a book which by no means proclaims itself a scientific work and whose author, out of sheer disgust at the unscientific way in which people trumpet up scientific method, would wish rather to be outside this hurly-burly, and is so far from pompously teaching trivialities that it is his joy to assume on the part of the reader the greatest possible amount of knowledge. If motion is allowed in relation to repetition in the sphere of freedom, then its development in this sphere is different from logical development in this respect, that *transi-*

tion is a becoming. In the sphere of logic transition is mute, in the sphere of freedom it *becomes.* So when possibility in logic qualifies itself as actuality it merely disturbs the hushed reticence of the logical process by talking about motion and transition. In the sphere of freedom, on the other hand, there is possibility, and actuality emerges as a transcendency. Therefore when even Aristotle said that the transition from possibility to actuality is a κίνησις he was not talking about logical possibility and actuality but about the possibility and actuality of freedom, and therefore he quite rightly posits motion." (IV B 117, pp. 288*ff.*)

Although this lengthy disputation with Heiberg was not published, S.K. felt the need of a public explanation, and therefore in *The Concept of Dread,* a book which he published the following year, he recapitulated a part of this in a footnote, which of course was attributed to Vigilius Haufniensis, the pseudonymous author of this work. This note ought to be available to readers of *Repetition*; and therefore I add it to the introduction.

Commenting upon a passage in *The Concept of Dread* which affirms that "sin belongs to the subject of ethics in so far as it is upon this concept ethics founders by the help of repentance," the note says:

"With regard to this point one will find several observations by Johannes de silentio author of *Fear and Trembling* (Copenhagen 1843). There the author several times allows the wishful ideality of the aesthetical to founder upon the exacting ideality of ethics, in order by these collisions to let the religious ideality come to evidence, which is precisely the ideality of reality, and therefore is just as desirable as that of aesthetics and not impossible like that of ethics, and to let it come to evidence in such a way that it breaks out in the dialectical leap and with the positive feeling, 'Behold all things have become new!' and in the negative feeling which is the passion of the absurd to which the concept of 'repetition' corresponds. Either the whole of existence is to be expressed in the requirement of ethics, or the condition for its fulfilment must be provided—and with that the whole of life and of existence begins afresh, not through an immanent continuity with the foregoing (which is a contradiction), but by a transcendent fact which separates the repetition from the first existence by such a cleft that it is only a figure of speech to say that the foregoing and the subsequent state are related to one another as the totality of living creatures in the sea are related to those in the air and on the land, although according to the opinion of some natural scientists the former is supposed to be the prototype which in its imperfection prefigures everything which becomes manifest in the latter. With regard to this category one may compare *Repetition* by Constantine Constantius (Copenhagen 1843). This book is in fact a whimsical book, as its author meant it to be, but nevertheless it is so far as I know the first which has energetically conceived 'repetition' and let it be glimpsed in its pregnance to explain the relation between the ethnical and the Christian, by indicating the invisible point and the *discrimen rerum* where science breaks against science until the new science comes forth. But what he has discovered he has hidden again by arraying the concept in the form of jest which appropriately offers itself as a mode of presentation. What moved him to do this it is difficult to say, or rather it is difficult to understand; for he says himself that he writes this 'so that the heretics should not be able to understand him.' As he has only wished to employ himself with this subject aesthetically and psychologically, he might have planned it all humoristically, and the effect would have been produced by the fact that the word at one moment signifies everything, and the next moment the most insignificant thing, and the transition, or rather the perpetual falling from the stars, is justified as a burlesque contrast. However, he stated the whole thing pretty clearly on page 53: 'Repetition is the *interest* of metaphysics and at the same time the interest upon metaphysics founders. Repetition is the solution in every ethical view; repetition is a *conditio sine qua non* of every dogmatic problem.' The first sentence contains an allusion to the thesis that metaphysics is disinterested, as Kant affirmed of aesthetics. As soon as the interest emerges, metaphysics steps to one side. For this reason the word *interest* is italicized. The whole interest of subjectivity emerges in real life, and then metaphysics founders. In case repetition is not posited, ethics remains a binding power; presumably it is for this reason he says that 'it is the solution in every ethical view.' If repetition is not posited, dogmatics cannot exist at all; for in faith repetition begins, and faith is the organ for the dogmatic problems. In the sphere of nature repetition exists in its immovable necessity. In the sphere of spirit the problem is not to contrive to get change out of repetition and find oneself comfortable under it, as though the spirit stood only in an external relation to the repetitions of the spirit (in consequence of which good and evil alternate like summer and winter), but the problem is to transform repetition into something inward, into the proper task of freedom, into freedom's highest interest, as to whether, while everything changes, it can actually realize repetition. Here the finite spirit falls into despair. This Constantine has indicated by stepping aside and letting repetition break forth in the young man by virtue of the religious. Therefore Constantine says several times that repetition is a religious category, too transcendent for him, that it is a movement by virtue of the absurd, and on page oo it is said that eternity is the true repetition. All this Professor Heiberg has failed to observe, but he has very kindly wished by his knowledge (which like his New Year's gift-book is singularly elegant and up to date) to help this work to become a tasteful and elegant insignificance, by pompously bringing the question back to the point where Constantine begins, bringing it to the point where (to recall a recent book) the aesthetic writer in *Either/Or* had brought it in 'The Rotation of Crops.' If Constantine were really to feel himself flattered by enjoying in this case the rare honor which brings him into an undeniably elect company—then to my way of thinking, since it was he who wrote the book, he must have become stark mad. But if on the other hand an author like him, who writes in order to be misunderstood, were so far to forget himself and had not ataraxia enough to account it to his credit that Professor Heiberg had not understood him—then again he must be stark mad. And this I do not need to fear, for the circumstance that hitherto he has not replied to Professor Heiberg indicates that he has adequately understood himself."

"Repetition" as a philosophic concept S.K. had already reached in his unfinished work of the previous year which he entitled *De omnibus dubitandum est* and ascribed to the pseudonym Johannes Climacus who was to figure as the author of the more strictly philosophic works, the *Fragments* and the *Postscript*. Here this concept is briefly but decisively stated, bringing it into relation, as he does here, with "interest." Cf. IV B 1, pp. 149*f*.*

If upon reaching the end of this book the reader should be perplexed or dismayed at finding no result—for S.K. and his pseudonyms are opposed on principle to giving any "results," and we are told simply that the young man "disappeared"—and if with human curiosity one would like to know the sequel, it really is told, though in a place where one would hardly look for it, namely, in the *Edifying Discourses* which were written to accompany this work. They were written later—yes, but it was only a few weeks later, and they were published on the same day. They therefore give us a view of the young man immediately after he disappeared from the sight of the psychologist Constantine across "the borders of the marvellous." You will recognize him even in the fragment I am about to quote, and you will see that he is still "in good hands."

"Then in turn it is the opposition of adversity which will

* *De omnibus dubitandum est* has been translated into English by T. H. Croxall and was published by the Stanford University Press, 1958.

strengthen such a one in the inward man. And why not? The inward man in fact proclaims himself in this man's deep concern; and adversity has precisely the effect of causing the outward, the visible, the tangible, to vanish and become confused. But does it then always call the inward to life? Adversity does indeed make every man anxiously concerned, but does it always make him concerned about God? Does not life often confirm the truth of the serious saying which is to be heard in the same passage which warns against prosperity and therefore deserves the more earnest heed: that adversities too are temptations? Behold the anxious man! Regard him more closely. Thou canst hardly recognize him again as the man who started out in life so joyful, so strong, so confident. His aim in life was so clear to him, so desirable, his thought approved his effort, his heart was set upon it, he relied upon his strength—and hope promised him a fortunate fulfilment. For there is a hope which is heaven's fatherly gift to the child, a hope with which youth goes forth into life. This hope sponsors everything he undertakes. Who then gave him this hope unless it was the Father in heaven? Should it not then be valid in the wide world, in all the kingdoms and lands which appertain to the heavenly King who gave him this hope? Yet it did not turn out thus, and soon adversity had wrested this beautiful hope from the strong and cheated the weak out of it. Then everything was confused before him. There was no longer a ruler in heaven, the wide world was the arena for life's wild alarms, there was no ear which gathered the confusion into an accord, no hand stretched out to take a guiding part. However a man might console himself in life, hope, he thought, was lost, and lost it remained. The more he stared down into the anarchy into which everything seemed to be resolved, the more might it acquired over him, till he was completely infatuated by it, his thought became dizzy, he himself plunged down into it, and he lost his self in despair. And even if the distress did no acquire so seductive a power over him, his soul nevertheless remained without sympathy and alien to everything. He beheld it like the others, but in everything he read an invisible writing declaring that it was emptiness and deception. Or he withdrew from men and like an assassin wore out his soul with griefs, with gloomy thoughts, in the fruitless service of restless moods. What was lacking to such a man? What was it he did not gain when he lost all? What but strengthening in the inward man?

"That man on the other hand in whose soul there was this distress before ever the distress approached him which comes from without, he whose soul never was so satisfied by joy but that it retained concern for the 'testimony,' nor so overwhelmed by the outward concern that the possibility of joy vanished so long as he was still concerned about the 'testimony'—to him the distress which comes from without became little by little a friend. It united with the concern within him, it prevented him from seeing life in a false light, it helped him to let the soul sink little by little into concern until it found the 'testimony.' Then little by little he became lighter and lighter, he cast off gradually the earthly weight of the worldly wish and reposed with the 'testimony' in God, blissful by reason of the hope which he had won. For there is a hope of which the Scripture says that it is acquired by hard probation. What probation does the Scripture mean? Why, that of course in which a man is assured of obtaining all that he hopes. The Scripture says that this probation is the fruit of the trial of temptation. But such a hope the world cannot take away, for it is gained indeed through distress and gains strength by distress. Opposition helped him then to be strong in the inward man; for he who has learned what he learned from what he suffered, and by what he suffered was taught the good, acquired not only the best teaching but what is much more . . . the best Teacher; and he who is taught by God is strengthened in the inward man. Then, though he had lost all, he would nevertheless have gained all—and Abraham possessed only a burial-place in the land of Caanan, and yet he was God's elect."*

If Schrempf had been patient enough to interpret S.K.'s position in the light of the *Edifying Discourses* which were expressly meant as an interpretation of his pseudonymous works, he would not perhaps have been so confident in affirming, as he did in his *Nachwort,* that S.K. got into trouble needlessly by taking too seriously Hegel's notion of "the universal," and got out of it by adopting blindly the Biblical notion of "trial" —that is to say, the naïve Old Testament picture of God tempting Abraham and Job in order to find out if they were really faithful, a notion which, as he rightly says, is inconsistent with the idea of an omniscient God. But really the Hegelian notion of "the universal" was not, as Schrempf understands it here, an abstract notion of mankind in general, but the ethical norm which applies not only universally but to every individual man. And the notion of "trial" is found also, though with a sublimer meaning, in the New Testament and in the words of Christ himself. S.K. in fact was very far from standing in need of the schooling Schrempf gives him when he informs him that there is a difference between the Old Testament and the New. An entry in the *Journal* shows that precisely at this time and in this connection he was reflecting profoundly upon this difference (IV A 143):

"That's the difficulty of it, that one has both the Old and the New Testament; for the Old Testament has entirely different categories. For what would the New Testament say to a faith which thinks it should get things quite to its liking in the world, in the temporal, instead of letting this go and grasping the eternal? Hence the inconstancy of the clerical address, according as the Old or the New Testament is transparent in it."

* All eighteen of the *Edfiying Discourses* are available in English translation by David F. and Lillian Marvin Swenson (Augsburg). Some of them—but not the one here quoted—can be found in the Harper Torchbook, TB/32.

I have on several occasions lapsed into a little polemic against Schrempf, although it might seem superfluous in America. But evidently there is some reason for it, for an anonymous writer in a German newspaper in America has abused me scornfully as an adherent of the "Bayreuth School." I confess I do not know the reason for that name, but it is further defined as the school of Geismar and Hirsch. I may add to it the name of Haecker. In fact there are no names with which I would more gladly be associated. Indeed I wonder what other names could be compared with them in Germany among the *viel-zu-Viele* who have written about Kierkegaard. They have cruelly thrown me into the briar patch—but like Br'er Rabbit that is where I like to be.

Princeton
April 26, 1941

REPETITION

An Essay In Experimental Psychology

BY

CONSTANTINE CONSTANTIUS

COPENHAGEN 1843
[October 16]

On wild trees the flowers are fragrant; on cultivated trees, the fruits.

FROM "STORIES OF HEROES" BY PHILOSTRATUS THE ELDER.

WHEN the Eleatic School denied the possibility of motion, Diogenes, as everybody knows, stepped forth as an opponent. He *stepped* forth literally, for he said not a word, but merely walked several times back and forth, thinking that thereby he had sufficiently refuted those philosophers. Inasmuch as for a long time I have been engaged, at least occasionally, with the problem whether a repetition is possible and what significance it has, whether a thing gains or loses by being repeated, it suddenly occurred to me, "Thou canst take a trip to Berlin, where thou hast been before, and convince thyself now whether a repetition is possible and what significance it may have." At home I had almost been brought to a standstill by the problem. Say what one will, it is sure to play a very important rôle in modern philosophy; for *repetition* is a decisive expression for what "recollection" was for the Greeks. Just as they taught that all knowledge is a recollection, so will modern philosophy teach that the whole of life is a repetition. The only modern philosopher who had an inkling of this was Leibnitz.[1] Repetition and recollection are the same movement, only in opposite directions; for what is recollected has been, is repeated backwards, whereas repetition properly so called is recollected forwards. Therefore repetition, if it is possible, makes a man happy, whereas recollection makes him unhappy—provided he gives himself time to live and does not at once, in the very moment of birth, try to find a pretext for stealing out of life, alleging, for example, that he has forgotten something.

The love of recollection is the only happy love, an author has said.[2] In that he is perfectly right, too—if one will only remember that it first makes a man unhappy. In truth, the love of repetition is the only happy love. Like that of recollection it has not the disquietude of hope, the anxious adventuresomeness of discoverers, nor the sadness of recollection; it has the blessed certainty of the instant. Hope is a new garment, starched and stiff and glittering, yet one has never had it on, and hence one does not know how it will become one and how it fits. Recollection is a discarded garment, which beautiful as it may be, does not fit, for one has outgrown it. Repetition is an imperishable garment, which fits snugly and comfortably, neither too tight nor too loose. Hope is a charming maiden but slips through the fingers, recollection is a beautiful old woman but of no use at the instant, repetition is a beloved wife of whom one never tires. For it is only of the new one grows tired. Of the old one never tires. When one possesses that, one is happy, and only he is thoroughly happy who does not delude himself with the vain notion that repetition ought to be something new, for then one becomes tired of it. It requires youth to hope, and youth to recollect, but it requires courage to will repetition. He who would only hope is cowardly, he who would only recollect is a voluptuary, but he who wills repetition is a man, and the more expressly he knows how to make his purpose clear, the deeper he is as a man. But he who does not comprehend that life is a repetition, and that this is the beauty of life, has condemned himself and deserves nothing better than what is sure to befall him, namely, to perish. For hope is an alluring fruit which does not satisfy, recollection is a miserable pittance which does not satisfy, but repetition is the daily bread which satisfies with benediction. When one has circumnavigated existence, it will appear whether one has courage to understand that life is a repetition, and to delight in that very fact. He who has not circumnavigated life before beginning to live will never come to the point of living; he who circumnavigated it but grew tired had a poor constitution; he who chose repetition really lives. He does not run after butterflies like a boy; nor does he stand on tiptoe to peer at the glories of the world, for he knows them. Neither does he sit like an old woman at the spinning wheel of recollection, but he goes his way confidently, rejoicing in repetition. Indeed, if there were no repetition, what then would life be? Who would wish to be a tablet upon which time writes every instant a new inscription? or to be a mere memorial of the past? Who could wish to let oneself be stirred by everything that is fleeting and new, which ever newly delights the effeminate soul? If God himself had not willed repetition, the world would never have come into existence. He would either have followed the light plans of hope, or he would have recalled it all and conserved it in recollection. This he did not do, therefore the world endures, and it endures for the fact that it is a repetition. Repetition is reality, and it is the seriousness of life. He who wills repetition is matured in seriousness. This is the vote I cast for my part, and it means also that it is far from being seriousness to sit on the sofa and pick one's teeth . . . and be somebody (for instance, Councillor of Justice), or to walk in the street with dignity . . . and be somebody (for instance, His Right Reverence), no more than it is life's seriousness to be a royal equerry. All such things are in my eyes only jest, and as such they are sometimes a poor enough jest.

The love of recollection is the only happy love, says an author who, so far as I am acquainted with him, is sometimes rather deceitful—not, however, in such a way that he might say one thing and mean another, but in such a way that he carries the thought to extremes, so that, if it is not grasped with the same energy, it appears the next moment to be something different. That saying is so expressed that it readily tempts one to admit that it is true, and then to forget that the saying itself is an expression for the profoundest melancholy, so that a melancholy so profound, and condensed in a single line, could not easily express itself better.

It was about a year ago I began to bestow serious attention upon a young man with whom already I had had some contact because his handsome appearance, the soulful expression of his eyes, almost tempted me—a certain toss of the head, a wantonness in his utterances, convinced me that he had a profound nature which possessed more than one register, whereas a certain insecurity of modulation indicated that he was in that seductive age when maturity of spirit announces itself, as does that of the body at a far earlier age by the change in the voice. By means of those careless advances which a coffee-house liking permits, I had already drawn him to me and taught him to regard me as a confidant whose talk in many ways enticed his melancholy from him in the form of outbursts, while I like a Farinelli[3] alluring the crazy king out of his gloomy retreat, could accomplish this without the use of tongs, because my friend was still young and pliable. Such was our relationship when about a year ago, as I said, he came up to me quite beside himself. His appearance was more vigorous than heretofore, his features more beautiful, his great glowing eyes had widened, in short, he was transfigured. When he informed me that he was in love, I reflected involuntarily that she must be a lucky girl to be loved in this fashion. He told me that he had already been in love for some time but had concealed it from me; now he had attained the goal of his desire, had declared his love and found it reciprocated. Although generally I am inclined to remain a detached observer in relation to people, it was impossible for me to be so with him. Say what you will, a young man deeply in love is something so beautiful that for very joy at the sight one forgets to observe. In general, deep human emotions in a person disarm the observer. Only where instead of these there is hollowness, or where they are coquettishly concealed, has one a desire to make observations. In case one were witness to the fact that a man was praying with his whole soul, who could be such a monster as to make observations? who would not rather feel himself pierced through by this outpouring of the man's devotion? When on the contrary one hears a parson declaim a well prepared sermon, wherein by an artfully constructed passage he several times testifies to the congregation (without any prompting on their part) that what he says is the simple faith, unskilled in elegant phrases, but capable of bringing forth by prayer that which (according to his affirmation, which presumably was well substantiated) he had in vain sought after in poetry, art and erudition—upon that, one calmly applies the microscope to one's eye and does not allow the ear to gulp down what is said, but pulls the blinds, the critical sieve which tests every note and every word. The young man of whom I speak was deeply and sincerely and beautifully and humbly in love. For a long while I have not been so delighted by anything as by looking at him. For it is often a dreary thing to be an observer, it makes one as melancholy as being a detective on the police force; and when an observer performs well the duties of his calling he is to be regarded as a police spy in a higher service, for the art of the observer is to bring hidden things to light. The young man talked about the girl with whom he was in love, but without employing many words. His talk was not an insipid appraisement, as a lover's eulogy often is. There was no self-importance in him, as though he were a shrewd fellow to have captured such a girl; there was no self-confidence; his love was wholesome, pure, unspoiled. He confided to me with charming candor[4] that the reason for his visit was his need of a confidant in whose presence he could talk aloud to himself, the more particular reason being that he was fearful of remaining all day with the girl and being burdensome to her. He had already started for her house several times but had compelled himself to turn away. He now asked me to take a drive with him, for the sake of diverting him and to make the time pass quicker. I was as willing as he; for from the moment he confided to me, he could be sure that I would be unconditionally at his service. I employed the half hour before the carriage came in writing several business letters, bidding him in the meantime fill his pipe and turn the pages of an album which lay on the table. Such occupation, however, he had no need of, he was sufficiently occupied with himself, was not even calm enough to sit down, but walked quickly back and forth across the floor. His gait, his movements, his gestures, were all eloquent, he himself glowed with love. As a grape when it is at the point of perfection becomes transparent and clear, while the juice bubbles through its fine veins, as the husk of a fruit breaks when the fruit ripens to all its fullness, so did love break forth almost visibly in his being. I could hardly forbear to snatch a sidewise glance at him now and then, almost as though I were in love with him; for such a youth is as alluring a sight as a young girl.

As it often is the way with lovers that they take refuge in the words of the poets in order to let love's sweet perturbation break out in blissful gladness, so it was in his case. As he paced back and forth across the floor he repeated again and again a verse of Poul Møller's

> To my arm-chair there comes a dream
> From the springtime of youth,
> A longing intense
> For thee, thou sun amongst women.

His eyes filled with tears, he flung himself down on a chair and repeated the verse again and again. Upon me this scene made a harrowing impression. Great God! thought I, such a melancholy has never before presented itself in my practice. That he was melancholy I knew well enough, but that a love affair could have such an effect upon him! And yet how consistent is every abnormal pyschic condition, if only it is normally present. People often proclaim that a melancholy man has only to fall in love, and then it all vanishes. If the man is really melancholy, how might it be possible for him not to be occupied with melancholy concern about that which to him is the most important concern of all? He was in love, deeply and sincerely in love; that was evident, and yet at once, on one of the first days of his engagement, he was capable of recollecting his love. Substantially he was through with the whole relationship. Before he begins he has taken such a terrible stride that he has leapt over the whole of life. Though the girl dies tomorrow, it will produce no essential change, he will again fling himself upon a chair, again his eyes will fill with tears, he will again repeat the words of the poet. What a strange dialectic! He longs for the girl, he has to restrain himself by force from hanging around her the whole day, and yet at the very first instant he has become an old man with respect to the whole relationship. There must be a misunderstanding at the bottom of it. Nothing for a long while has moved me so much as this scene. That he would become unhappy was clear enough, and that the girl too would become unhappy was no less clear, although it is not at once possible to foresee in what way this would occur. This much, however, is certain, that if anybody can take a hand in talking about the love of recollection, that young man can. Recollection has the great advantage that it begins with the loss, hence it is secure, for it has nothing to lose.

The carriage had come. We drove up along the coast, with the intent of seeking later the real woodland roads. Since against my will I had begun to behave toward him as an observer, I could not resist trying all sorts of experiments to take the log, as sailors say, of the headway of his melancholy. I struck all possible erotic chords. No. I tried the effect of the changing environment. In vain. Not the bold immensity of the sea, nor the lulling stillness of the forest, nor the enticing solitude of evening, could draw him out of the melancholy longing by which he was not so much drawing near to the beloved as forsaking her. His mistake was incurable, and his mistake was this, that he stood at the end instead of at the beginning. But such a mistake is certainly a man's undoing.

And yet I maintain the correctness of his mood as an erotic mood, and the man who in his experience of love has not experienced it thus precisely at the beginning, has never loved. Only he must have another mood alongside of this. This potentiated act of recollection is the eternal expression of love at the beginning, it is the token of a real love. But on the other hand an ironic elasticity is requisite in order to be able to make use of it. This he lacked, his soul was too soft for it.

It must be true that one's life is over at the first instant, but there must be vitality enough to kill this death and transform it into life. In the earliest dawn of love the present and the future strive one with another in order to acquire an eternal impression, and this act of recollection is precisely the counter-current of eternity flowing back into the present—provided this recollection is healthy.

We returned home, and I took leave of him; but my sympathy was almost too powerfully set in motion, I could not get rid of the thought that in a very short time this must lead to a dreadful explosion.

In the course of a fortnight I saw him off and on in my home. He himself began to be aware of the misunderstanding. The young girl whom he adored had become almost a burden to him; and yet she was his darling, the only woman he had ever loved, the only one he would ever love. On the other hand, nevertheless, he did not love her, he merely longed for her. For all this, a striking change was wrought in him. There was awakened in him a poetical productivity upon a scale which I had never thought possible. Then I easily comprehended the situation. The young girl was not his love, she was the occasion of awakening the primitive poetic talent within him and making him a poet. Therefore he could love only her, could never forget her, never wish to love anyone else; and yet he was forever only longing for her. She was drawn into his very nature as a part of it, the remembrance of her was ever fresh. She had meant much to him, she had made him a poet, and thereby she had signed her own death warrant.

As time went by his situation became more and more agonizing. His melancholy attained more and more the ascendancy, his physical force was consumed in psychic struggles. He perceived that he had made her unhappy, and yet he was aware of no fault; but precisely the fact of being innocently guilty of her unhappiness was to him a stumbling-block which wrought up his passion to the wildest agitation. To admit to her how the matter stood, would, as it seemed to him, mortify her most deeply. This indeed would be the same as telling her that she was an incomplete being, that he had outgrown her, that he no longer had need of the rung of the ladder on which he had climbed. What then would the consequence be? Knowing that he would not love anyone else, she would become his sorrowing widow, who lived only upon the memory of him and of their relationship. He could not make any confession. For her sake he was too proud to do that. His melancholy ensnared him more and more, and he resolved to keep up the falsification. His entire poetic talent was now employed to entertain and delight her. What might have served bountifully for many was all lavished upon her; she was and remained his darling, the only one whom he adored, although he was near losing his mind with agonizing dread at the monstrous untruth which only served to imprison her more and more. In reality her existence or nonexistence was in a certain sense of no importance to him, only it was his melancholy which found delight in rendering life enchanting to her. That she was blissful goes without saying, for she had no suspicion, and the nutriment offered her was only too savory. He did not desire to be productive in the stricter sense; wherefore he held his productivity under the shears, as he said, and cut the flowers as a bouquet for her. She had no suspicion. Of that I am sure. And indeed it would be revolting if a young girl could be selfish enough to take a man's melancholy in vain. However, such a case can occur, and once I was very near discovering an instance. Nothing is more seductive to a young girl than to be loved by a poetically melancholy nature. And if she merely has enough egotism to imagine that she proves the fidelity of her love by clinging to him instead of giving him up, she has a very easy task in life, which permits her to enjoy not only the reputation and consciousness of being faithful, but also the most finely distilled sentiment of love. God preserve a man from such fidelity!

One day he came to my house. His gloomy passions had

gained complete ascendancy. In the wildest outburst he cursed existence, his love and the darling girl. From that moment he came to my house no more. Presumably he could not forgive himself for having admitted to another person that the girl had become a torment to him. With that he had spoiled for himself everything, even the joy of sustaining her pride and making her a goddess. When he encountered me he avoided me, and if we met he never talked, though evidently he made an effort to appear joyful and confident. I was considering how I could follow him up more closely, and to that end had begun to get on the track of his subordinate associates. When one has to do with a melancholy person, one often gets to know most by the help of subordinates. Before a serving-man or woman, an old family retainer, one often reveals oneself more freely than to associates who are closer in culture and outward condition. I knew a melancholy man who went through life like a dancer and deceived everybody, myself included, until by means of a barber I got on another trace. This barber was an elderly man who lived in straitened circumstances and served his customers himself. Compassion for the barber's need moved the gay man to let his melancholy manifest itself, and the barber knew what no one else suspected. However, the young man spared me this trouble; for he had recourse to me again, although he was firmly resolved never to set his foot inside my door. He proposed that I should meet him in solitary places at a definite time. I was willing; and to that end I bought two tickets of admission to the fish-ponds in the city moat. There we met early in the morning. At the hour when the day is warring with the night, when even at midsummer a cold shiver runs through nature, there we met in the damp morning mist and on the dewy grass, and the birds flew up affrighted at his outcry. At the hour when the day has conquered, when every living thing rejoices in existence, at the hour when the darling young girl whom he coddled by his pain lifted her head from the pillow and opened her eyes because the god of sleep who had been sitting by her couch arose, at the hour when the god of dreams laid his finger upon her eyelids so that she dozed off again into a brief slumber, while he related to her what she never had guessed, and related it so softly, in words scarcely breathed, that she had forgotten it all when she awoke—at that hour we separated again. And whatever the god of dreams confided to her, at least she did not dream what passed between us. What wonder the man was pale! What wonder that I am, who was his confidant, and the confidant of many like him!

Again some time passed. I really suffered a great deal on account of the young man, who was fading away daily. And yet I did not in the least regret participating in his sufferings, for in his love at least the idea was stirring. (And after all one does sometimes see such a love in real life, God be praised! though in romances and novels one seeks it in vain.) Only when such is the case has love any significance; and the man who is not enthusiastically convinced that the idea is the vital principle in love, and that for this, if need be, one must sacrifice life, yes, what is more, sacrifice even love itself, however practical reality may favor it—such a man is banned from poetry. On the other hand, where love is supported by the idea, every movement, every fleeting emotion even, is not without significance, because the essential is always present, the poetic collision, which, as I well know, can be far more terrible than in the case I am here describing. But the service of the idea (which does not mean in the case of love to serve two masters) is also an exacting service, for no reigning beauty can be as exigent as the idea, and no girl's displeasure can be so heavy as the disapproval of the idea, which is the more terrible because it can never be forgotten.

If I were to pursuc in detail the moods of the young man as I learned to know them, not to speak of including in a poetical manner a multitude of irrelevant matters—salons, wearing apparel, beautiful scenery, relatives and friends—this story might be drawn out to yard lengths. That, however,

I have no inclination to do. I eat lettuce, it is true, but I eat only the heart; the leaves, in my opinion, are fit for swine. I prefer with Lessing[5] the rapture of conception to the labor of childbirth. If there is anybody who has anything to say against this, let him say on, it makes no difference to me.

Time passed. When I was able to do so I attended that nocturnal service where he with wild outcries got all the exercise he needed for the whole day, for he employed the daytime by enchanting the girl. As Prometheus, chained to the rock while the vulture pecked at his liver, was able to captivate the gods by his divination, so did he captivate the loved one. Each day the whole thing was carried to the highest pitch, for every day was the last. But it could not continue thus. He bit the chain which bound him, but the more his passion foamed, the more blissful was his song, the more tender his speech, the more galling the chain. To construct a real relationship out of this misunderstanding was impossible for him, it would have meant to make her the victim of an eternal deception. To explain to her the mistake by letting her know that she was only the visible semblance, whereas his thought, his soul, was seeking something else which he transferred figuratively to her—that would mortify her so deeply that his pride revolted against it. That was a method which he despised above all others. And he was right in that. It is despicable to deceive and seduce a girl, but it is still more despicable to desert a girl in such a way that one does not even become a scoundrel but makes a more brilliant retreat by putting her off with the explanation that she is not the ideal, and consoling her with the notion that she was only one's muse. Such a thing can easily be done when a man has some practice in talking a girl around; in the hour of need she will accept the proposal, and one gets out of it very well, remaining a moral man, even an amiable one, and afterwards she is more essentially dishonored than if she *knew* she had been deceived. Therefore in every love relationship which cannot be realized although it has been begun, delicacy of behavior is the most offensive thing, and he who has an eye for the erotic and is not a coward can readily see that to be indelicate is the only means he has left to keep the girl in a good state of preservation.

In order if possible to put an end to these sufferings, I exhorted him to venture energetically upon the extremest measures. It was merely necessary to find a point of unity. So I made to him the following proposal. "Bring everything to naught, transform yourself into a despicable person who finds pleasure only in duping and deceiving people. If you can do this, then equality is brought about, for then there would be no longer any question of an aesthetic difference which would give you a superior right as against her, something which people are often inclined to concede in the case of so-called extraordinary individualities. She will then be the victorious one and be absolutely in the right—you absolutely in the wrong. Do not do it, however, too suddenly, for that would merely inflame her love. Try first if possible to be a bit disagreeable to her. Do not tease her. That is an incitement. No, be capricious, with a propensity to twaddle; do one thing one day and another the next, but without passion, in a routine sort of way, which does not, however, degenerate into inattention to her, for the outward show of attention must be just as great as ever, though altered to a perfunctory demonstration lacking in all sincerity. Instead of a genuine inclination of love, you are constantly to exhibit a certain nauseous quasi-love which is neither indifference nor desire. Let all your behavior be as disagreeable as it is to see a man slobber. Do not begin, however, unless you have strength to carry the thing through, otherwise it is a stalemate; for there is no one so shrewd as a young girl, when it is a question, that is, of knowing whether she is loved or not; and there is no operation so difficult as that in which one has to make use of the extirpating knife, an instrument which as a general thing only time knows rightly how to wield. Then when everything is under way, you have only to turn to me, and I shall manage the rest. Let the rumor be spread abroad that you have a new love affair, of a sort rather unpoetic; for otherwise you will only incite her. I know very well that such a thing could not occur to your mind, for it is well understood between us that she is the only one you love, although it is impossible for you to translate the purely poetic relationship into real love. There must be some truth to substantiate the rumor, and that I shall take care of. I am looking up here in town a girl with whom I shall strike an agreement."

It was not merely consideration for the young man which prompted me to lay this plan, for I cannot deny that I gradually came to regard his lady-love with a prejudiced eye. That she should notice nothing whatever, that she had no suspicion whatever of his suffering and of what might well be the reason of it, that if she suspected it she did nothing, made no effort to save him by giving him the one thing he needed and which she alone could give him, namely, his freedom, which would save him if precisely she was the one who gave it; for by that act of magnanimity she would acquire ascendancy over him and would not be mortified. I can forgive a girl everything else, but I can never forgive her for mistaking the task of love. When a girl's love is not sacrificial, she is no woman but a masculine figure, and so I shall always take delight in suffering her to fall a victim to revenge or to laughter. And what a theme for a comic poet, to let such a lovelorn maiden, who had first like a vampire sucked the blood of her lover, until in his distress and despair he broke with her—to let such an inamorata come upon the stage as an Elvira[6] who sings with acclaim in this rôle accompanied by the lamentations of relatives and friends, an Elvira who is prima donna in the chorus of deceived maidens, who can talk with emphasis about the faithlessness of men, a faithlessness which evidently will cost her her life, an Elvira who performs all this with so much aplomb and assurance that it does not occur to her for half a second that her faithfulness was rather calculated to take the life of her lover. Great is the fidelity of women, especially when it is declined; unfathomable and inconceivable it is at all times. The situation would be priceless if her lover, in spite of all his distress, had preserved enough humor not to waste a word of wrath upon her but contented himself with the profounder revenge of duping her and confirming her in the false notion that she was shamefully deceived by him. In case this is the way with her, I warrant her that if the young man is capable of carrying out my plan, it will give her a dreadful shock, and yet not without poetic justice. For she is convinced that she is doing the best she can, and yet this fact, if she is egotistic, will make the chastisement all the harder. He handles her with all possible erotic consideration, and yet his method is precisely calculated to cause her the greatest pain, if she is egotistic.

He was willing to enter into my plan and approved of it without reserve. In a *magasin de modes* I found what I sought, a right pretty girl whose future I promised to provide for if she would enter into my plan. He was to show himself with her in public places and visit her at hours which would leave no doubt that they were living on an understanding with one another. To that end I engaged a dwelling for her in a house which had an entrance upon two streets, so that he had only to walk through the house late in the evening in order to give certainty to maid-servants etc. and start gossip going. Now that everything was arranged, I had only to see to it that the lady-love did not remain unaware of his new relationship. The little seamstress wasn't so bad, but of such a sort that the lady-love, all jealousy apart, might be astonished that a girl like this was preferred above her. If I had only had the lady-love in view, the seamstress might have been rather different; but as I knew nothing with certainty about the lady, and as I did not want to play a prank upon the young man, I made my choice in the interest of his method.

The seamstress was engaged for one year. The relationship with her must last as long as that in order to dupe the loved one completely. During that period he was to work himself free from his poetic existence. If he succeeded in this, a *redintegratio in statum pristinum*[7] might be brought about. In the course of that year the young girl also (this was a matter of great importance) would have opportunity to work herself out of the relationship, for he had not honored her with an uncertain intimation of the possible result of such an operation. If it were to come about that she, when the moment of repetition arrived, had grown tired—well, then, he had at least acted magnanimously.

In this way everything was in readiness. I already held the string in my hand, and my soul was extraordinarily intent upon the outcome. He failed to appear, I never saw him again. He did not have strength to carry out the plan.[8] His soul lacked the elasticity of irony. He had not the strength to take irony's vow of silence, not the power to keep it; and only the man who keeps silent amounts to anything. Only he who really is able to love is a man, and only he who is able to give his love whatsoever expression it may be is an artist. In a certain sense it perhaps was well that he did not begin the thing, for he hardly could have supported the terrors of the adventure, and from the beginning I was a little fearful because he had need of a confidant. He who knows how to keep silent discovers an alphabet which has just as many letters as the one commonly in use, so that he can express everything in this thieves' Latin, so that there is no sigh so profound that he has not the laughter which corresponds to it in thieves' Latin, and no prayer so importunate that he has not the witticism which redeems the claim. For him there will come an instant when it is as though he were about to lose his reason. But this is only a moment, though it is a dreadful moment. It is like the fever which comes on of nights at half past eleven or twelve, and at one o'clock one works as buoyantly as ever. If one endures this madness, one is sure to conquer.

But here I sit and relate in full detail what really was adduced in order to show that the love of recollection does indeed make a man unhappy. My young friend did not understand repetition, he did not believe in it, and did not desire it with energy. What made his fate so hard was the fact that he really loved the girl, but in order to love her really he must first be clarified out of the poetical confusion into which he had fallen. He might have made this confession to the girl. When one wants to dismiss a young girl that is a perfectly reputable method. That, however, he did not wish to do, and I thoroughly agreed with him that it was not the correct thing. He thereby would have cut her off from the possibility of existing under her own auspices, and also exempted himself from becoming perhaps an object of her contempt, and from the breathless dread of never being able to indemnify her for what she had lost.

If the young man had believed in repetition, of what might he not have been capable? What inwardness he might have attained!

However, I have anticipated and got further along than I meant to. My aim was merely to present the first moment, when it became clear that the young man was in a true sense the woeful knight of the only happy love of recollection. The reader will permit me perhaps to reflect once more upon the instant when intoxicated with recollection, he strode into my room, when his heart thoroughly "*ging ihn über*"[9] in that verse of Poul Møller's, when he confided in me that he must deny himself in order not to sit beside his beloved the whole day long. That same verse he repeated the evening we parted. It will ever be impossible for me to forget that verse, indeed the recollection of his disappearance[10] I could more easily erase from my mind than the memory of that instant; and it is true also that the report of that event alarmed me less than did the earlier situation. That is the way I am built. At the first shudder of presentiment my soul has in an instant followed through the whole chain of consequences, which in reality often require a long lapse of time to come to evidence.

The concentration of presentiment one never forgets. So it is, I believe, an observer ought to be built, but when he is built in this fashion he will also suffer much. The first moment may overwhelm him almost to the point of fainting, but in this fit of pallor the idea has impregnated him, and from now on he is in an apt mood for discovery. When a man does not possess this feminine quality which permits the idea to come into the right relation to him, which always is a fructifying relation, he is of no use as an observer, for he who does not discover the totality discovers nothing.

When we parted that evening, and he thanked me for helping him to while away the time which passed all too slowly for his impatience, I then thought to myself, "Was he perhaps candid enough to report all this to the young girl, with the result presumably that she loves him more dearly than ever?" I wonder if he did so. If he had asked my advice, I should have counseled him against it. I had said to him, "Hold firm at the beginning, from a purely erotic point of view that is the wisest course, unless your soul is so serious that you can direct her thought to something far higher." If he told her that, he did not behave wisely.

He who has some opportunity to observe young girls and to give ear to their conversation has likely often heard this formula: "N.N. is a good man, but he is tiresome; on the other hand F.F. is so interesting and piquant." Whenever I hear these words in the mouth of a little maiden I always think, "You ought to be ashamed of yourself. Is it not pitiful that a young girl should talk in this fashion?" If a man has run wild in the interesting, who might save him, unless it were precisely a young girl? Is she not culpable if she does not do it? Either the person in question is not capable of playing the rôle of the interesting, and then it would be indelicate to require it of him; or he can do it, and then . . . , for a young girl ought to be prudent enough never to elicit the interesting; the girl who does that always loses, as seen from the vantage point of the idea, for the interesting does not lend itself to repetition; she who does not do it is always victorious.

Six years ago I was on a journey of forty miles out in the country and stopped at an inn to take my midday dinner. I had partaken of an acceptable and savory meal, was in rather gay spirits, and was just standing with a cup of coffee in my hand and inhaling its odor, when at that instant a young and pretty girl passed the window and turned into the court belonging to the inn. From this I drew the conclusion that she wanted to go down into the garden. One is young . . . so I gulped down the coffee, lit a cigar, and was just on the point of following the beckoning of fate and the footsteps of the girl when there was a knock at my door and in walked . . . the young girl. She bowed to me pleasantly and asked if it was not my carriage which was waiting in the court, whether I was not going to Copenhagen, and whether I would permit her to ride with me. The modest and yet genuinely feminine dignity with which she made the request was enough to make me instantly lose sight of the interesting and piquant. And yet to ride forty miles with her in one's own carriage, with coachman and valet, having her entirely in my power, is in fact far more interesting than meeting a girl in a garden. Nevertheless it is my conviction that even a more frivolous man than I would not have felt tempted. The confidence with which she entrusted herself to my keeping is a better defense than all a girl's shrewdness and cunning. We rode together. She could not have been safer if she were riding with a father or brother. I remained silent and reserved; only when it appeared that she would make a remark was I responsive. My coachman had orders to make haste. There was a rest of five minutes at each post-station. I alighted with hat in hand and asked if she would order any refreshment, my valet standing behind me with hat in hand. When we approached Copenhagen I had the coachman turn into a side road, and there I alighted to walk two miles into the city, in order to spare her the possibility of meeting an acquaintance, or any similar incident which might cause her embarrassment. I have never inquired who she was, where she dwelt, or what was the occasion of her sudden journey; but she has always been to me a pleasant recollection, which I have never permitted myself to offend by even the most innocent curiosity.—A girl who craves the interesting becomes the trap in which she herself is caught. A girl who does not crave the interesting believes in repetition. Honor to her who is such by nature, honor to her who became such in time.

I must ever be repeating that it is with reference to repetition I say all this. Repetition is the new category which has to be brought to light. If one knows something of modern philosophy and is not entirely ignorant of the Greek, one will easily perceive that precisely this category explains the relation between the Eleatic School and Heraclitus, and that properly it is repetition which by mistake has been called mediation. It is incredible how much fuss has been made about mediation in the Hegelian philosophy, and how much foolish patter has under this caption enjoyed honor and repute. One would do better to subject mediation to a searching examination and so render a little justice to the Greeks. Their treatment of the doctrine of "being" and "nothingness," their treatment of "the instant," of "non-being" etc.,[11] trumps Hegel. Mediation is a foreign word; repetition [i.e. *Gentagelse*] is a good Danish word and I congratulate the Danish language upon having a good philosophical term. In our time no explanation is forthcoming as to how mediation comes about, whether it results from the movement of the two factors, and in what sense it already is contained in them, or whether it is something new which supervenes, and if so, how. In this respect the Greek reflection upon the concept of κίνησις[12] which corresponds to the modern category of transition, deserves the utmost attention. The dialectic of repetition is easy; for what is repeated has been, otherwise it could not be repeated, but precisely the fact that it has been gives to repetition the character of novelty. When the Greeks said that all knowledge is recollection they affirmed that all that is has been; when one says that life is a repetition one affirms that existence which has been now becomes. When one does not possess the categories of recollection or of repetition the whole of life is resolved into a void and empty noise. Recollection is the pagan life-view, repetition is the modern life-view; repetition is the *interest* of metaphysics, and at the same time the interest upon which metaphysics founders; repetition is the solution contained in every ethical view, repetition is a *conditio sine qua non* of every dogmatic problem.

Let everyone pass what judgment he will upon what I have said with regard to repetition, let him also pass what judgment he will upon the fact that I say it here in this way, expressing myself after Hamann's[13] example "in divers tongues" and speaking the language of Sophists, of quibbles, of Cretans and Arabians and Creoles, babbling indifferently *rebus* and principles, arguing now *κατ' ἀνθωπον*, now *κατ' ἐξοχην*. Assuming that what I say is not a sheer lie, I would do better perhaps to send my straw-thought[14] to a systematic appraiser, perhaps something might come of it, a note in the System perhaps—proud thought! Then I should not have lived in vain!

As for the significance which repetition has in a given case, much can be said without incurring the charge of repetition. When in his time Professor Ussing[15] made an address before the 28th of May Association and something in it met with disapprobation, what then did the professor do? Being at that period always resolute and *gewaltig*, he pounded on the table and said, "I repeat it." So on that occasion his opinion was that what he had said gained by repetition. A few years ago I heard a parson deliver on two successive Sundays exactly the same discourse. If he had been of the opinion of the professor as he ascended the pulpit on the second occasion he would have pounded the desk and said, "I repeat what I said last Sunday." This he did not do, and he gave no hint of it. He was not of Professor Ussing's opinion—and who knows if the professor himself be still of the opinion that it was an advantage to his discourse to be repeated again? At a court reception when the Queen had told a story, and all the courtiers had laughed, including a deaf minister, who then arose and craved permission to tell his story . . . and told the same one—the question is what was his view of the significance of repetition? When a schoolteacher says in class, "I repeat that Jaspersen must sit still," and the same Jaspersen gets a bad mark for repeated disturbance, the significance of repetition is exactly the opposite.

However, I will dwell no longer upon such examples but will proceed to tell a little about the voyage of discovery I undertook in order to investigate the possibility and the significance of repetition. Without letting anybody know about it (lest all the gossip might render me inept for the experiment and create a disgust for repetition), I went by steamer to Stralsund, and there took a seat in a diligence for Berlin. Among the learned there are various opinions as to which seat in a diligence is the most comfortable. My *Ansicht* is that it is misery for the whole crowd. On my previous journey I had the end seat inside the carriage near the front (some consider this a great prize), and then for thirty-six hours was so shaken together with my nearest neighbors, all too near, that upon reaching Hamburg I had not merely lost my mind but lost my legs too. We six persons who sat inside the carriage were kneaded into one body, and I had a lively sense of what had happened to the people of Mol,[16] who after they had been sitting together for a long time could not distinguish their own legs. In order at least to be a member of a smaller body I chose a seat in the coupé. It was a change. Nevertheless everything was repeated. The postillion blew his horn, I closed my eyes, resigned myself to despair, and thought, as I am accustomed to do on such occasions, "God knows whether thou wilt ever reach Berlin, and in that case whether thou wilt ever become a man again, capable of emancipating thyself in the individuality of isolation, or whether thou wilt retain the memory that thou art a member of a greater body."

I arrived in Berlin after all, and hastened at once to my old lodging[17] in order to convince myself how far a repetition might be possible. I can assure every sympathetic reader that on my first visit I succeeded in getting one of the most agreeable apartments in Berlin, and this I can now affirm with the more confidence because I have seen many. Gendarmes Square is surely the most beautiful in Berlin. The theater and the two churches make a fine appearance, especially as viewed from a window by moonlight. The recollection of it contributed much to hasten my steps. One ascends a flight of stairs in a house illuminated by gas, one opens a small door, one stands in the vestibule. On the left is a glass door leading to a cabinet. One goes straight ahead, one finds oneself in an antechamber. Beyond this are two rooms entirely alike and furnished entirely alike, with the effect of seeing one room doubled in a mirror. The inner room is tastefully lighted. A branch candlestick stands on the writing table, beside which stands a handsome armchair covered with red velvet. The first room is not illuminated. Here the pale light of the room is blended with the stronger illumination from the inner room. One sits down upon a chair by the window, one looks out upon the great square, one sees the shadows of pedestrians hasten along the walls. Everything is transformed into a theatrical decoration. A dreamy reality looms up in the background of the soul. One feels a desire to throw on a cloak and slink quietly along the walls with a searching glance, attentive to every sound. One does not do it, one merely sees oneself doing it in a renewed youth. One has smoked one's cigar, one retires to the inner room and begins to work. Midnight is past. One extinguishes the candles, one lights a small night lamp. The moonlight triumphs unalloyed. A single shadow appears still darker, a single footstep takes a long time to disappear. The cloudless vault of heaven seems sad and meditative, as though the end of the world were past and heaven undisturbed were concerned only with itself. One goes out again into the antechamber, into the vestibule, into that little cabinet, one goes to sleep—if one is of that fortunate number that can sleep.

But, alas, here no repetition was possible. My host, materialist that he was, *hatte sich veränd ret,* in the pregnant sense in which the Germans use this word, and as it is used in some quarters of Copenhagen, if I am correctly informed, in the sense of getting married. I wanted to wish him good fortune; but as I have not sufficient command of the German language to be able to turn a sharp corner, nor had promptly at my disposition the phrases appropriate to such an occasion, I confined myself to pantomimic motions. I laid my hand upon my heart and looked at him, while tender sympathy was legibly depicted upon my countenance. He pressed my hand. After we had thus come to an understanding with one another he proceeded to prove the aesthetic validity of marriage.[18] In this he was extraordinarily successful—just as he was formerly in proving the perfection of the bachelor life. When I am talking German I am the most compliant person in the world.

My former host was eager to serve me, and I was eager to lodge with him; so I took one chamber and the vestibule. When I came home the first evening and had lit the candles, I thought to myself, "Alas, alack, is this repetition?" I was in a sadly depressed mood, or if you prefer to say so, I was in a mood precisely appropriate to the day; for fate had strangely contrived that I arrived in Berlin on the first day of Lent, a day of universal fasting and penitence. It is true they did not cast dust in one's eyes, with the words *Memento, o homo, quod cines est et in cinerem rivertaris,*[19] but nevertheless the whole city was one cloud of dust. I thought at first that it was all arranged by the government, but later I was convinced that the wind had made itself responsible for this and without respect of persons was following its whim or its evil habit; for in Berlin at least every other day is Ash Wednesday. But the dust has little relevance to my subject. This discovery had nothing to do with "repetition," for on my previous visit I had not observed this phenomenon, presumably because it was winter.

When one has got comfortably and snugly settled in one's

dwelling, when one has thus a fixed point from which to dart out, a safe hiding-place where one can retire to devour one's prey in solitude (something I prize in particular, because like certain beasts of prey I cannot eat when anybody is looking on)—then one makes oneself acquainted with the sights of the city. If one is a traveller *ex professo,* a globetrotter who travels on the scent of everything others have scented out, or in order to write the names of the principal sights in his diary, or his own name in the register of guests, then one engages, a *Lohndiener* and buys *Das ganze Berlin* for 4 *Groschen.* By my method one remains an impartial observer whose declaration ought to be taken on faith in every police protocol. On the other hand, if one is travelling without any pressing pretext, one may do as one pleases, see once in a while something which others have not seen, overlook the important things, and get a casual impression which has significance only for oneself. Such a carefree vagabond generally has not much to recount to others, and if he does it he readily runs the risk of impairing the good opinion good people have formed of his virtuousness and morality. If a man had journeyed abroad for a long time and had never been *auf der Eisenbahn,*[20] ought he not to be expelled from all good society? What if a man had been in London and had never taken a ride in the Tunnel! What if a man were to come to Rome, fall in love with a small corner of the town which offered him inexhaustible material for delight, and were to leave Rome without having seen one single sight!

Berlin has three theaters. What is presented at the Opera House in the way of operas and ballets is said to be *grossartig*; what is presented at the Dramatic Theater is supposed to be for instruction and culture, not merely for pleasure.[21] About that I do not know. But I know that in Berlin there is a theater called Königstäter Theater. The official tourists visit it rather rarely, although (and this is also significant) somewhat more frequently than the sociable places of refection on more retired streets where a Dane can refresh his memory of Lars

Mathiesen and Kehlet.[22] When I arrived in Stralsund and read in the newspaper that "The Talisman"[23] was to be performed in that theater I was at once in good humor. The recollection of it awakened in my soul, and the first time I saw it I felt as though this first impression merely evoked in my soul a recollection which pointed far back in time.

Surely there is no young man with any imagination who has not at one time been captivated by the enchantment of the theater, and desired to be himself carried away into the midst of that fictitious reality in order to see and hear himself as an *alter ego,* to disperse himself among the innumerable possibilities which diverge from himself, and yet in such a way that every diversity is in turn a single self. Of course it is only at a very early age such a desire can express itself. Only the imagination is awake to this dream of personality, all the other faculties are still sound asleep. In such a dream of imagination the individual is not a real figure but a shadow, or rather the real figure is invisibly present and therefore is not content with casting one shadow, but the individual has a multiplicity of shadows, all of which resemble him and for the moment have an equal claim to be accounted himself. The personality is not yet discovered, its energy announces itself only in the passion of possibility; for it is true in the life of the spirit as it is in the case of many plants that the germinal sprout comes last. However, this shadow existence also demands its satisfaction, and it never is good for a man if he does not get time to live out his life, although on the other hand it is pitiful or comic when an individual lives himself out in this way. The pretension of such a man to be a real man is just as dubious as the demand of immortality on the part of people who are not in a position to make their appearance personally at the Day of Judgment, but delegate in their stead a deputation of good intentions, ephemeral resolutions, half-hour plans etc. The essential thing is that everything happens at the right time. Everything has its time in youth, and what has had its time there gets it again later; and it is just as wholesome for an older man to have in his life a past whereby he is in debt to laughter, as to have a past which exacts tears.

When in a mountainous region one hears the wind day in and day out execute firmly and unchangingly the same theme, one perhaps is tempted for an instant to ignore the imperfection of the analogy and to rejoice in this symbol of the consistency and assurance of human freedom. One perhaps does not reflect that there was a moment when the wind, which now for many years has had its dwelling-place among these mountains, came to this region as a stranger, flung itself wildly, meaninglessly into the fissures, into the caverns, producing now a piercing shriek by which it almost startled itself, now a hollow roar from which it had itself to flee, now a note of lamentation, without knowing itself from whence it came, now a sigh drawn from the anguish of the abyss, so profound that the wind itself was for an instant afraid and doubted if it dared to dwell in these regions, and now a lyrical and frolicsome note of gladness—until, after it had learnt to know its instrument, it brought all this into accord in the melody which from day to day it executes unchangeably. So does the possibility of the individual stray at random amongst its own possibilities, discovering now one and now another. But the possibility of the individual does not want merely to be heard; it is not merely an onrushing force like the wind, it also assumes shape, therefore at the same time it wants to be seen. Every possibility of the individual is therefore a sounding shadow. The cryptic individual no more believes in the great noisy feelings than he does in the crafty whisper of malice, no more in the blissful exultation of joy than in the infinite sigh of sorrow; the individual only wants to hear and see with pathos, but, be it observed, to hear and see himself. However it is not really himself he wants to hear. That is not practicable. At that instant the cock crows, and the figures of the twilight flee away, the voices of the night fall silent. If they continue, then we are in an entirely different domain, where all this goes on under the alarming observation of moral responsibility, then we are on the border of the demoniacal. In order not to get an impression of his real self, the cryptic individual requires that the environment be as light and ephemeral as the figures, as the frothy effervescence of the words which sound without echo. Such an environment is the theatrical stage, which for this reason precisely is appropriate to the shadow-play of the cryptic individual. Among the shadows in which he discovers himself, whose voice is his voice, there is perhaps a robber chieftain. He must recognize himself in the mirrored image, in the robber's manly figure, his swift but piercing glance, the signature of passion written legibly upon his furrowed countenance, nothing must be lacking. He must lie in ambush in the mountain pass, he must be listening for the movement of travellers, he must blow his whistle, the whole band rushes down; his voice must dominate the turmoil; he must be cruel, order all to be cut down, and turn away from the massacre with indifference, but he must be chivalrous toward the frightened girl, etc., etc.

A robber has in fact his home in the gloomy forest. If one were to deposit in such a place that fantastic hero of the footlights, were to provide him with all the equipment he needed, and beg him merely to keep still long enough for one to get several leagues away, before giving himself over to his passionate rage—I think he would remain completely dumb. It would turn out with him perhaps as it did with a man who several years ago honored me with his literary confidence. He came to me lamenting that he was to such a degree overwhelmed by fullness of ideas that it was impossible for him to put down anything on paper, because he could not write fast enough. He begged me to be so kind as to be his secretary and write at his dictation. I at once smelled a rat and promptly consoled him with the assurance that I could write as fast as a runaway horse, since I wrote only a letter of each word and yet guaranteed that I could read everything I had written. My willingness to be of service knew no bounds. I had a big table brought out, numbered many sheets of paper, in order that I might not even waste time in turning a page, laid out a dozen steel pens with their holders, dipped my pen—and the man began his address as follows: "Well, yes, you see, my dear Sir, what I really wanted to say was . . ." When he was through with the address I read it aloud to him, and from that time he has never asked me to be his secretary.

That robber would presumably find the scale too big for him, and yet in another sense too little. No. Measure out for him a *coulisse* with one tree, hang before it a lamp, which makes the illumination even stranger, and with that this forest is even bigger than the real forest, bigger than the primeval forests of North America, and yet he can penetrate it with his voice without becoming hoarse. This is the sophistical pleasure of imagination, to have thus the whole world in a nutshell, which is bigger than the whole world, and yet not bigger than the individual can fill.

Such an inclination for theatrical acting and expectorating by no means evinces a call to be an actor. Where there is such a call the talent shows itself at once as a disposition for this particular art, and even the richest talent of this sort which awakens in a man has not so broad a compass as the inclination we have been considering. This inclination is merely immaturity of imagination; for it is quite another matter when it has its ground in vanity and an inclination to shine. Then the whole thing has no deeper ground than vanity, a ground unfortunately which may be very deep.

Although in the individual life this inclination vanishes in time, yet it is reproduced in a riper age when the soul has seriously collected itself. Yes, although the art of the theater is perhaps not serious enough for the individual, he may perhaps have pleasure in turning back occasionally to that first state and rehearsing it in sentiment. He wishes now to be affected comically, and to be himself in a comically productive relation to the theatrical performance. Therefore, though neither tragedy nor comedy can please him, precisely because of their perfection, he turns to the farce.[24]

The same phenomenon recurs also in other spheres. One

sometimes sees a mature individual, sated with the strong meat of reality, who remains unaffected by a painting executed with artistic skill. On the other hand he may be moved at seeing a Nürnberg print[25] in color, such a picture as not long ago was commonly to be found in the shops. There one sees a landscape which depicts a country scene in general. This abstraction is one which cannot be represented artistically. The effect therefore has to be attained by indirection, that is, by depicting a concrete subject casually selected. And yet I would ask every man whether from such a landscape he does not get the impression of a country scene in general, and whether this category is not left over from the days of childhood. From the days of childhood when one had such prodigious categories that now one is almost made dizzy by them, when from a piece of paper one cut out a man and a woman, which were man and woman in general, and that in a stricter sense than Adam and Eve were. A landscape painter, whether he strives to produce an effect by a faithful rendering of the subject, or by a more ideal reproduction, perhaps leaves the individual cold, but such a picture as I have in mind produces an indescribable effect for the fact that one does not know whether to laugh or cry, and because the whole effect depends upon the mood of the beholder. There is surely no person who has not passed through a period when no wealth of language, no passion of exclamation was sufficient for him, when no expression, no gesticulation satisfied, when nothing contented him except to break out with the strangest leaps and somersaults. Perhaps the same individual learned to dance, perhaps he often saw ballets and admired the art of the dancer, perhaps there came a time when the ballet no longer affected him, and yet he had moments when he could retire to his room, give himself up entirely to his impulse, and feel an indescribably humoristic relief in standing upon one leg in a picturesque attitude, or in consigning the whole world to death and the devil, and accomplishing it all by an entrechat.

At the Königstäter Theater they give farces, and of course

the audience is exceedingly diversified. Anyone who desires to make a pathological study of laughter at different social levels and as it is affected by diversity of temperament ought not to miss the opportunity afforded by the performance of a farce. The jubilation and clangor of the gallery and second tier is something quite different from the applause of a cultivated and critical public; it is a steady accompaniment, without which the farce could not be performed at all. The action generally takes place in the lower spheres of society, therefore the gallery and the second tier promptly recognize themselves, and their shouts and bravos do not express an aesthetic appreciation of the individual actors, but rather a purely lyrical explosion of their sense of contentment; they are not in the least conscious of being an audience, but want to take part in what is going on down in the street, or wherever the scene is laid. However, since this is impossible because of the distance, they behave like children who are merely permitted to see from a window a row in the street. The first tier of boxes and the *parterre* are also convulsed by laughter, although this is essentially different from the national yells of the Cimbro-Teutonic race, and even within this select sphere there are infinite nuances in the quality of the laughter, far more than at the performance of the best vaudeville. Whether one is disposed to regard this as a perfection or an imperfection, it is simply the fact. Every attempt at an aesthetic definition which might claim universal validity founders upon the farce, which is by no means capable of producing a uniformity of mood in the more cultured part of the audience. For, since the effect depends in great part upon the spontaneous creative activity of the spectator, the single individual asserts himself to an unusual degree, and in his own enjoyment is emancipated from the aesthetic obligation to admire, laugh, be touched, etc., according to the prescription of tradition. To view a farce is for a person of culture like playing the lottery, except that one is spared the annoyance of winning money. But such uncertainty is not what theater-goers generally want; hence they neglect the farce, or look down upon it loftily, which is all the worse for them. The real theatrical public has in general a certain narrow-minded seriousness; it wants (or at least imagines that it wants) to be ennobled and educated at the theater, it wants to have had (or at least to imagine that it has had) a rare aesthetic enjoyment; it would like to be able, as soon as it has read the posters, to know in advance how the thing is going to turn out this evening. Such an accord between promise and performance is impossible in the case of the farce; for the same farce may make many different impressions, and it may happen strangely enough that it has the least effect when it is best acted. One cannot therefore rely upon one's neighbors or upon the newspapers in order to know whether one has been entertained or not. This matter the individual must determine for himself, and no critic has as yet succeeded in prescribing a ceremonial for the public which deigns to see a farce; in this field no *bon ton* can establish itself. The reciprocal regard of actors and audience, which commonly gives one such a sense of security, is here done away with; one may be thrown into the most unexpected moods at seeing a farce, and therefore never can know with assurance whether one has behaved in the theater as a worthy member of society, and has laughed or wept at the appropriate place. One cannot admire as a conscientious spectator the fine characterization which is to be expected in a drama, for all the characters in the farce are sketched on the abstract scale of "the general." The situation, the action, the lines, are all on this scale. One can therefore quite as well be moved to sadness as convulsed by laughter. Irony is ineffectual in the farce, everything is naïve, and therefore the spectator as a single individual must be spontaneously active; for the *naïveté* of the force is so illusory that it is impossible for a cultivated person to be naïve in his attitude toward it. But in his spontaneous reaction to the farce consists in great part the entertainment of the individual, and he must venture to enjoy it without looking to the right or to the left or to the newspapers to find a guarantee that he really has been entertained. On the other hand, for the cultivated person who at the same time is free and easy enough to entertain himself independently, and has enough self-confidence to know by himself, without seeking the testimony of others, whether he has been entertained or not, the farce will have perhaps a very special significance, because it will affect his spirit in various ways, now by the spaciousness of the abstraction, now by the introduction of a palpable reality. But of course he will not bring with him a ready-made mood and let everything produce its effect in relation to that, but he will have cultivated his spirit to perfection and will keep himself in the state where not one single mood is present but the possibility of all.

At the Königstäter Theater they present farces, and to my mind excellent ones. My opinion is of course entirely individual, and I urge it upon no one, deprecating as I do every urgency applied to me. To be able to perform a farce with complete success the troupe must be composed in a special way. It must possess two (or at the most three) actors who have decided talent, or rather, creative genius. They must be the children of caprice, intoxicated with laughter, dancing for sheer humor and merriment. Although at other times, even a moment earlier, they are entirely like other people, yet the very instant they hear the bell of the stage manager they become transformed, and like the noble Arabian steed begin to puff and snort, their distended nostrils witnessing to the chafing spirit within them, wanting to be off, wanting to disport themselves wildly. They are not so much reflective artists who have made a study of laughter as they are lyrical geniuses who plunge into the abyss of laughter and then let its volcanic force cast them up upon the stage. They have therefore hardly calculated what they will do, but let the instant and the natural force of laughter be responsible for everything. They have courage to do what the ordinary man dares to do only when he is alone by himself, what the crazy man does in the presence of all, what the genius knows how to do with the authority of genius. They know that their exuberant mirth has no bounds, that the capital they possess of the comic is inexhaustible and almost every instant a surprise even to them; they know that they are capable of keeping the laughter going the whole evening, without more effort than it costs me to scribble this on paper.

When a theater possesses two geniuses of this sort it has enough for a farce, three is the greatest number admissible, for by more geniuses the effect is weakened, just as a man may die of hypertrophy. The other members of the troupe do not need to be talented, it is not even advantageous that they should be. Nor do the other members need to be engaged with an eye to the canons of beauty, they had better be assembled haphazard. All the rest of the troupe may well be as heterogeneous as that company which founded Rome, according to a drawing by Chodowiecki.[26] No one need be excluded even on the ground of physical deformity. On the contrary, such an anomaly would contribute notably to the success of the piece. Though one were bow-legged or knock-kneed or too much overgrown or stunted in growth, in short, if in one respect or another he is a defective example of the species, he can very well be used in the farce, and the effect he produces is incalculable. After the ideal comes in the very next place the accidental. A wit has said that one might divide mankind into officers, serving-maids and chimney-sweeps. To my mind this remark is not only witty but profound, and it would require a great speculative talent to devise a better classification. When a classification does not ideally exhaust its object, a haphazard classification is altogether preferable, because it sets imagination in motion. A tolerably true classification is not able to satisfy the understanding, it is nothing for the imagination, and hence it is to be totally rejected, even though for everyday use it enjoys much honor and repute for the reason that people are in part very stupid and in part have very little imagination. When at the theater one would have a representation of a man, one must either require a concrete form corresponding absolutely to the ideal, or else be content with the fortuitous. Those theaters which are "not merely for pleasure" ought to provide the former. Nevertheless one is content if in this case the actor is a handsome fellow with an advantageous figure and a good stage-face and a good voice. But this rarely satisfies me, for his acting awakens *eo ipso* the critical spirit, and as soon as that is awakened it becomes neither possible to determine what is required for being a man, nor easy to satisfy one's demands—and in this anyone will agree with me if he reflects that Socrates, in spite of the fact that his strong point was knowledge of men and self-knowledge, said[27] of himself that he did not know definitely whether he was a human being or a beast even more changeable than Typhon. On the other hand, in the case of a farce, the subordinate actors produce their effect by means of that abstract category "in general" and attain this by a fortuitous concretion. With this one has got no further than to reality. Nor should the actor seek to go further; but the spectator is reconciled comically by seeing this fortuitous concretion claiming to be the ideal, which it does by treading into the fictitious world of the stage. If an exception is to be made with respect to any of the subordinate actors, this must be in favor of the lady-love. Of course she must not by any means be a finished actress, yet in making the choice one ought to see to it that she is attractive, that her whole appearance in the rôle is charming and pleasant, that she is agreeable to look upon, agreeable, let us say, to have around.

The troupe at the Königstäter Theater is pretty much what I would desire. If I were to make any objection, it would apply to the subordinate actors, for against Beckmann[28] and Grobecker I have not a word of complaint. Beckmann is the perfection of a comic genius, who lyrically runs wild in the comic, does not distinguish himself by characterization but by effervescence of spirit. He is not great in the artistically commensurable but admirable in the individual incommensurable. He has no need of the support of team-play, of scenery and arrangement; precisely because he is in form he brings everything with him, at the same time that he is in an ecstasy of wantonness he paints the scenery for himself as well as any painter could. What Baggesen[29] says of Sara Nickels, that she rushes upon the stage with a country landscape behind her, applies in a good sense to Beckmann, only he is able to come walking. In the artistic theater properly so called one seldom sees an actor who can really walk and stand. I have seen, however, one single instance, but what Beckmann is capable of I have never before beheld. He not only can walk but he can *come walking*. This ability to "come walking" is a very different thing, and by this stroke of genius Beckmann improvises the scenic environment. He not only can represent a wandering apprentice lad, he can come walking like him, and that in such a way that one sees the whole thing, through the dust of the highway one espies a smiling village, hears its subdued din, sees the footpath which winds yonder down to the pond where it turns off at the smithy—when one sees Beckmann come walking with his little bundle on his back, his walking-stick in his hand, carefree and indefatigable. He is capable of coming on the stage with the street-urchins following him—which one does not see. Even Dr. Ryge[30] in "King Solomon and George the Hatter" could not produce this effect. Indeed Herr Beckmann is a pure economy for a theater, for when it possesses him it has no need of street-urchins or painted scenery. However this young apprentice is no characterization; for that the figure is too hastily sketched in its truly masterly contours, it is an incognito in which dwells the mad demon of laughter, which soon disengages itself and carries the whole thing off with unbridled mirth. In this respect Beckmann's dancing is incomparable. He has sung his couplet, now the dance begins. What Beckmann dares to do is perilous; for presumably he does not think himself competent in the strictest sense to produce an effect by his dancing attitudes. He is now beside himself. The madness of laughter within him can no longer be contained either in mimicry or in *réplique,* only to take himself like Münchausen by the nape of the neck and abandon himself to crazy caprioles, is consonant with his mood. The ordinary man, as I have said, may very well recognize what assuagement is to be found in this, but it requires indisputable genius to do it on the stage, it requires the authority of genius, otherwise it is pitiable.

Every burlesque actor must have a voice which is audible from behind the scenes, so that he can thus prepare the way for himself. Beckmann has a capital voice, which of course does not mean the same thing as a good vocal organ. Grobecker's voice is more strident, but one word from him behind the scenes produces the same effect as three flourishes of the trumpets on the festival of Dyrehavsbakken,[31] it predisposes one to laughter. In this respect I give him the preference, even over Beckmann. Beckmann's fundamental superiority consists in a certain indomitable common sense in his wantonness, and it is through this he attains to frenzy. Grobecker, on the other hand, sometimes rises to frenzy through sentimentality and a languishing mood. So it is I remember seeing him play in a farce the part of a steward who by reason of his devotion to his noble masters and by virtue of his faith in the importance of festal preparations for embellishing their life is engrossed with the thought of celebrating their lordships' arrival by a rustic fête. Everything is in readiness. Grobecker has chosen to represent Mercury. He has not altered his costume as steward, he has merely attached wings to his feet and put a helmet on his head, he assumes a picturesque attitude upon one leg, and begins his address to their lordships. Grobecker is not so great a lyrical artist as Beckmann, nevertheless he too is on good lyrical terms with laughter. He has a certain tendency toward correctness, and in this respect his acting is often masterly, especially in dry comedy, but he is not such a fermenting ingredient in the farce as is Beckmann. A genius he is nevertheless, and a genius for farce.

One enters the Königstäter Theater. One takes one's seat in the first tier of boxes; for here there are relatively few people, and when one is to see a farce one must be seated at one's ease, without feeling in the remotest way embarrassed by the solemn pretense of art which causes many to let themselves be jammed into a theater to see a play as if it were a question of their eternal salvation.[32] The air in this theater is also fairly pure, not contaminated by the sweat of an audience moved by sensibility to art, or by the finer emanations of art connoisseurs. In the first tier of boxes one can be fairly sure of getting a box alone by oneself. If that is not the case, I recommend to the reader (in order that he may at least get some profitable knowledge from what I write) the choice of boxes 5 and 6 on the left. There one finds at the very back a seat in a corner which is calculated for only one person, where one is incomparably well off. One sits there alone in one's box, and from this position the theater appears empty. The orchestra plays an overture, the music resounds in the hall rather uncannily for the reason that the theater is so empty. One has not gone to the theater as a tourist, or as an aesthetic spirit, or as a critic, but if possible as though it were a matter of no importance, and one is content with being well and comfortably installed, almost as well as in one's own room. The orchestra has finished, the curtain already rises a little, then begins that other orchestra which does not obey the conductor's baton but follows an inner impulse, that other orchestra, the voice of nature in the gallery, which already has sensed Beckmann behind the stage. I generally sat far back in the box and therefore could not see the second row of boxes and the gallery which like a visor projected beyond my head. All the more marvellous was the effect of this din. Wherever I was able to see, there was empty space for the most part, the vastness of the theater was transformed into the belly of the sea-monster in which Jonah sat, the noise in the gallery was like a movement of the monster's viscera. From the moment the gallery has begun its music no other accompaniment is necessary, Beckmann inspires it, and it him.

My nursery maid never to be forgotten, thou fugitive

nymph which hadst thy dwelling in the brook which ran past my father's farmstead and didst ever take a helpful part in the child's play, although thou wast only looking after thyself! Thou faithful comforter who throughout the years hast preserved thy innocent purity, hast ever remained young, whereas I have become old; thou quiet nymph to whom again I had recourse when I was weary of men, weary of myself, so that I needed an eternity to repose; when I was sorrowful, so that I needed an eternity to forget. Thou didst not deny to me that which men would deny me by making eternity just as busy and even more terrible than time.[33] There I lay by thy side and vanished from before my own eyes into the prodigious expanse of heaven above my head, and forgot myself in thy lulling murmur. Thou my happier self, thou fugitive life which dwellest in the brook which runs by my father's farmstead, where I lie outstretched as though my body were a discarded pilgrim's staff, but I am saved and liberated by thy melancholy purling.—Thus it was I lay back in my loge, cast aside like the clothing of a bather, flung beside the stream of laughter and merriment and jubilation which foamed past me incessantly. I could see nothing but the vast expanse of the theater, hear nothing but the din in the midst of which I dwelt. Only now and then did I raise myself, look at Beckmann and laugh so heartily that for very fatigue I sank down again beside the foaming stream. This in itself was blissful, and yet I sensed the lack of something. Then in the desert which I beheld about me I discovered a figure which gladdened me more than the sight of Friday gladdened the heart of Robinson. In a box directly opposite me was a young girl, seated in the third row, half hidden by an older lady who sat in the first row. The young girl evidently was not in the theater in order to be seen—as in fact in this theater one is in a great measure dispensed from the sight of these disgusting feminine exhibitions. She sat in the third row, her dress was simple and plain, almost a house dress. She was not wrapped in sable and marten but was enveloped in a big cloak, and projecting from its folds her head was graciously bowed, as the topmost bell of the lily-of-the-valley is bowed above the great enveloping leaves. When I had looked at Beckmann and let the laughter convulse my whole body, when I had sunk back in fatigue and suffered myself to be carried away by the stream of shouting and merriment, and when I stepped out of this bath and returned to myself, then my eyes sought her, and the sight of her refreshed my whole being by its friendly mildness. And when in the farce itself a more pathetic mood cropped up, then I looked at her, and her nature bestowed upon me resignation to bear the pathos, for through it all she sat with perfect self-repose, with her quiet smile of childlike wonder. Like me she came there every evening. Sometimes I fell to thinking what could have brought her, but these thoughts too remained merely sentiments which were like feelers after her, so for an instant it seemed to me as if she might be a girl who had suffered much and now wrapped herself closely in her shawl and would have nothing more to do with the world, until the expression of her face convinced me that she was a happy child who hugged herself in her cloak in order to enjoy herself thoroughly. She did not suspect that she was seen, and still less that my eye was watching over her; this would have been a sin too against her, and the worse for me; for there is an innocence, an unconsciousness, which even the purest thought may embarrass. One does not oneself discover such a thing, but when one's good genius confides to one where such a primitive soul of retirement lies hidden, then let him not offend it or grieve its genius. If she had felt merely a presentiment of my mute gladness, half fallen in love with her, all would have been spoilt, not to be made good again even by her whole love.

I know where there dwells several leagues from Copenhagen a young girl; I know the large shady garden with the many trees and shrubs; I know where a little way off there is a bank overgrown with brushwood, from which one can peer into the garden while hidden by the thicket. I have never confided this to anyone, not even my coachman knows it, for I deceived him by alighting some distance away and walking to the left instead of to the right. So when my soul is sleepless and the sight of my couch frightens me more than an instrument of torture, more than the patient fears the operating-table, then I drive the whole night. Early in the morning I take hiding in the thicket.Then when life begins to stir, when the sun opens its eye, when the birds flutter their wings, when the fox sneaks out of its hole, when the peasant stands at his door and looks out over the meadow, when the milkmaid goes pail in hand down into the meadow, when the reaper hammers his scythe resoundingly and rejoices in this prelude which is to be the refrain of the day and of his labor, then the young girl too comes forth. Who could sleep? Who could sleep lightly so that sleep itself would not be a heavier burden than that of the day? Who could arise from his bed as if no one had been lying upon it, so that the bed itself was cool and delicious and refreshing to behold, as if the sleeper had not rested upon it but only leaned over to put everything to rights? Who could die in such a way that even one's deathbed the very instant one is lifted from it was more inviting to behold than if a careful mother had beaten the bed and puffed it up so that the child might sleep more soundly? Then the young girl comes forth, then she walks about wonderingly (which wonders most, the girl or the trees?), then she stoops down and plucks fruit from the bushes, then she skips about lightly, then she stands still in thought. What marvellous eloquence there is in all this! Then my soul at last finds rest. Happy girl! If ever a man should win thy love, would that thou mightest make him as happy by doing everything for him as thou hast made me by doing nothing for me.

"The Talisman" was to be performed at the Königstäter Theater. The memory of it awoke in my soul, it all stood as vividly before me as when I left the theater the last time. I hastened to the theater. There was no box to be had for me alone, not even in those numbered 5 and 6 on the left. I had to go to the right. There I encountered a society which didn't know definitely whether it should enjoy itself or be bored. Such a company one can definitely regard as boring. There were hardly any empty boxes. The young girl was not to be seen, or else she was there and I could not recognize her because she was in company. Beckmann was unable to make me laugh. I held out for half an hour and then left the theater. "There is no such thing as repetition," I thought. This made a profound impression upon me. I am not so very young, nor altogether unacquainted with life, and already long before I came to Berlin the last time I had weaned myself from the habit of counting upon uncertainties. Nevertheless I still believed that the enjoyment I once had in that theater ought to be of a more durable kind, precisely for the reason that before one could really get a sense of what life is one must have learnt to put up with being disappointed by existence in many ways, and still be able to get along—but surely with this modest expectation life must be the more secure. Might existence be even more fraudulent than a bankrupt? After all, he pays back 50 percent or 30 percent, at least he pays something. The comical is after all the least one can demand—cannot even that be repeated?

With these thoughts in my mind I went home. My writing-table was in the accustomed place. The velvet armchair still existed. But when I saw it I was so exasperated that I was near breaking it to bits—all the more because everybody in the house had gone to bed, and there was no one to take it away. What is the good of a velvet armchair when the rest of the environment doesn't correspond with it? It is as if a man were to walk naked wearing a cocked hat. When I had gone to bed without having had a single rational thought it was so light in the room that I constantly saw the velvet armchair, whether awake or in my dreams, so when I got up next morning I carried into effect my resolution and had it thrown into a storeroom.

My home had become cheerless, precisely because it was the

reverse of a repetition, my mind was unfruitful, my troubled imagination was engaged in transmuting into the delights of Tantalus the memory of how richly the thoughts presented themselves on the former occasion, and this rank weed of memory strangled every thought at birth.

I went out to the coffee-house, where on the previous visit I went every day to enjoy the drink which according to the words of the poet,[34] if it is "pure and warm and strong and not abused," can be placed alongside of that with which the poet compares it, namely, "friendship." I insist at least upon good coffee. Perhaps the coffee was just as good as before, one might almost suppose so, but I didn't like it. The sun blazed hotly upon the window of the shop, the place was stuffy, pretty much like the air in a casserole, fit to stew in. A draft like a small trade-wind penetrated everywhere and forbade me to think of any repetition, even if an opportunity had presented itself.

That evening I went to the restaurant where I used to go on my former visit, and where, presumably by force of habit, the food agreed with me. When I went there every evening I was acquainted with it most accurately; I knew how the early guests when they were on the point of leaving greeted the fraternity they parted from, whether they put on their hats in the inner room, or in the last room, or only when they opened the door, or not till they were outside. Nothing escaped my observation. Like Proserpine[35] I plucked a hair from every head, even the bald ones.—It was always the same, the same jokes, the same courtesies, the same expressions of comradeship; the locality in all respects the same, in short, "the same in the same."[36] Solomon says that "the contentions of a wife are like a continual dropping," which would apply to this still-life. Dreadful thought! Here a repetition was possible!

The next night I was at the Königstäter Theater. The only thing repeated was the impossibility of repetition. In the Unter den Linden the dust was insupportable, and every attempt to press in among the people and wash off the dust with a human bath was discouraging in the highest degree. However I turned and twisted, it was in vain. The little *danseuse* who had formerly enchanted me by her grace, which consisted so to say in a leap, had taken the leap. The blind man outside the Brandenburger Thor, my harpist (for I was surely the only one who was concerned about him) was wearing a coat of mixed gray, instead of light green which corresponded with my sad longing, for it made him look like a weeping willow. He was lost for me and won for the universal human. The beadle's much admired nose had turned pale. Professor A. A. wore a new pair of trousers which imparted to him an almost military air. . . .

When this experience had been repeated for several days I became so exasperated, so tired of repetition, that I resolved to make my way home again. My discovery was of no importance, and yet it was a strange one, for I discovered that there is no such thing as repetition, and I had convinced myself of this by trying in every possible way to get it repeated.

My hope was set upon my home. Justinus Kerner[37] tells somewhere of a man who was tired of his home, that he had his horse saddled in order to ride forth into the wide world. When he had gone a little distance his horse threw him. This turn of events was decisive for him, for when he turned to mount his horse his eye lit again upon the home he wished to leave, and he looked, and behold! it was so beautiful that he at once turned back. In my home I could reckon with tolerable certainty upon finding everything ready for repetition. I have always had a great distrust of upheavals, indeed I go so far that for this reason I even hate any sort of cleaning, and above all household scrubbing. So I had left the severest instructions to have my conservative principles maintained even in my absence. But what happens! My faithful servant held a different opinion. He reckoned that if he commenced the commotion soon after my departure, it surely would have ceased before my return, and he was surely man enough to put back everything punctiliously in its place. I arrive, I ring the doorbell, my servant opens. That was a momentous moment. My servant became as white as a corpse, and through the half-opened door I saw the most dreadful sight: everything was turned upside down. I was petrified. My servant in his consternation did not know what to do, his evil conscience smote him, and he slammed the door in my face. That was too much, my distress had reached its climax, I might expect the worst, to be taken for a ghost, like Commerzienrat Grünmeyer.[38] I perceived that there is no such thing as repetition, and my earlier view of life triumphed.

How ashamed I am of myself that I who had been so cavalier with that young man have now got just as far, indeed it seems to me as though I were that young man, as though my big words, which now I would not repeat for any price, were only a dream from which I awakened to let life take back again insistently and perfidiously all that it gave, without giving a repetition. And is it not true that the older one gets, the more deceptive life proves to be, that the shrewder one becomes and the more ways one learns to help oneself, the worse scrapes one gets into. A little child cannot help himself at all, yet always slips through easily. I remember once seeing on the street a nursemaid pushing a perambulator in which there were two children. One of them was hardly a year old, had fallen asleep and showed no sign of life. The other was a little girl of about two years, stout and chubby and with short arms, quite like a diminutive worthy matron. She had shoved herself forward in the baby-carriage till she occupied by good measure two-thirds of the space, and the smaller child lay by her side as if it were a bag my lady had brought with her. With an egotism worthy of admiration she did not deign to be concerned about anybody but herself or about any human affairs, if only she could procure a good place. Then came a runaway cart, the baby-carriage was in evident danger, people came running up, by a quick movement the nurse steered the carriage into a safe harbor; everybody present was alarmed, including myself. Through all this the little miss sat perfectly tranquil, and without changing her expression continued to pick her nose. She thought, presumably, "What has that to do with me? It's the nurse's affair." Such heroism one seeks in vain among grown-up people.

The older one grows and the more understanding of life one acquires, and taste for the agreeable and ability to relish it, in short, the more competent one becomes, the less one is content. Content—entirely and absolutely and in every way content—one never becomes, and to be tolerably content is not worth the trouble, so it is better to be entirely discontented. Everyone who has thoroughly considered the matter will agree with me that it is never granted to a man in his whole life, even for so much as for half an hour, to be absolutely content in all imaginable ways. That for this more is required than having food and clothing, I surely do not need to say.[39]

Once I was very close to it. I got up in the morning feeling uncommonly well. This sense of well-being increased out of proportion to all analogy during the forenoon. Precisely at one o'clock I was at the highest peak and surmised the dizzy maximum which is not indicated on any scale of well-being, not even on the poetical thermometer. The body had lost all its earthly heaviness, it was as though I had no body, just for the reason that every function enjoyed its completest satisfaction, every nerve tingled with delight on its own account and on account of the whole, while every pulsation, as a disquietude in the organism, only suggested and reported the sensuous delight of the instant. My gait became a glide, not like the flight of a bird that cleaves the air and leaves the earth behind, but like the billows of the wind over a field of grain, like the yearning bliss of the cradling waves of the sea, like the dreamy gliding of the clouds. My very being was transparent, like the depths of the sea, like the self-contented silence of the night, like the quiet monologue of midday. Every feeling of my soul composed itself to rest with melodious resonance. Every thought proffered itself freely, every thought proffered itself with festal gladness and solemnity, the silliest conceit not less than the richest idea. Every impression was surmised before it arrived and was awakened within me. The whole of existence seemed to be as it were in love with me, and everything vibrated in preordained *rapport* with my being. In me all was ominous, and everything was enigmatically transfigured in my microcosmic bliss, which was able to transform into its own likeness all things, even the observations which were most disagreeable and tiresome, even disgusting sights and the most fatal collisions. When precisely at one o'clock I was at the highest peak, where I surmised the ultimate attainment, something suddenly began to chafe one of my eyes, whether it was an eye-lash, a mote, a speck of dust, I do not know; but this I know, that in that selfsame instant I toppled down almost into the abyss of despair—a thing which everyone will understand who has been so high up as I was, and when he was at that point has been engaged with the generic question how nearly absolute contentment can be attained. Since that time I have given up every hope of ever feeling myself content absolutely and in all ways, have given up the hope I once cherished, not indeed of being absolutely content at all times, but at least at particular instants, even if these units of instants were not more numerous than, as Shakespeare says,[40] "a tapster's arithmetic was capable of summing up."

I had got so far as to entertain this modest hope before I learned to know that young man. As soon as I asked myself, or somebody raised a question, about perfect contentment, though it be but for half an hour, I always "renounced" the play. Then it was that time and again I conceived the idea of repetition and grew enthusiastic about it—thereby becoming again a victim of my zeal for principles. For I am thoroughly convinced that, if I had not taken that journey for the express purpose of assuring myself of the possibility of repetition, I should have diverted myself immensely on finding everything the same. What a pity that I cannot keep to the ordinary paths, that I will have principles, that I cannot go clad like other men, that I will walk in stiff boots! Are not all orators, both the religious and the secular, both sea captains and undertakers, both heroes and cowards—are they not all in agreement that life is a stream? How then can one get so foolish an idea as that of repetition, and, still more foolishly, erect it into a principle? My young friend thought, "Oh, well, let it go," and therewith he was better off than if he had begun with repetition. For with that he would likely have got his lady again, as did the lover in the ballad who wanted repetition—he would have got her again as a nun, with hair cut short and with blanched lips. He wanted repetition, therefore he got it, and repetition killed him.

Das Nönnlein kam gegangen
In einem schneeweissen Kleid;
Ihr Här'l war abgeschnitten,
Ihr roter Mund war bleich.

Der Knab, er setzt sich nieder,
Er sass auf einem Stein;
Er weint die hellen Tränen,
Brach ihm sein Herz entzwei.*

Hail to the post-horn! That is my instrument—for many reasons, and principally for this, that one never can be sure of eliciting from this instrument the same note. And he who puts it to his mouth and deposits his wisdom therein can never be guilty of repetition; and he who instead of making answer to his friend holds out to him a post-horn with a polite request to use it, though he says nothing, has explained all. This is my symbol. As the ascetics of old placed a skull upon the table and by the contemplation of it directed their meditations, so shall the post-horn upon my table always remind

* Herder, *Volkslieder*, Leipzig 1825, Vol. I, p. 57.

me of what the significance of life really is. Hail to the post-horn! But travel is not worth the pains; for one need not budge from the spot in order to be convinced that there is no repetition. No, he sits tranquilly in his room; for if all is vanity and passes swiftly away, he travels more rapidly than by railway, notwithstanding that he himself is sitting still. Everything shall remind me of this, my servant shall wear the livery of a postillion, and I myself will not drive to a dinner party except in a diligence. Farewell, farewell, thou rich hope of youth! Why dost thou hasten so impetuously? What thou art chasing does not exist, and thou thyself just as little. Farewell, thou manly strength! Why dost thou paw the ground so fiercely? That on which thou treadest is a vain imagination. Farewell, thou victorious purpose! Thou art near enough to the goal, for thou canst not take thy works with thee without turning back, and that thou canst not do. Farewell, farewell delight of the forest! When I desired to see thee thou wast withered. Ride on thou fleeting river! Thou alone dost know what thou wilt, thou who hast only the desire to run and lose thyself in the sea, which never becomes full. Go on thou spectacle upon the stage of life, which no one calls a comedy, no one a tragedy, because no one knows the end! Thou theater of existence where life is not given back to one any more than money is! Why did no one ever return from the dead? Because life does not know how to captivate as death does, because life does not possess the power of persuasion which death possesses. Yea, death possesses marvellous powers of persuasion; if only one will not contradict it but will let it have its say, then it persuades in an instant, so that never has anyone had a word to object or longed for the eloquence of life. O death, strong is thy power of persuasion, and next to thee no one is able to talk so beautifully as the man whose eloquence procured him the name of πεισιθάνατος,[41] because with the power of eloquence he talked of thee.

REPETITION[42]

SOME time passed. My servant, like a domestic Eve, had made reparation for his earlier offense. A monotonous and uniform order was restored in my whole household economy. Everything which was not able to move stood in its precise place, and what was able to go went its accustomed way —my parlor clock, my servant, and myself who with measured tread walked back and forth across the floor. For though I had convinced myself that no such thing as repetition exists, yet it is a sure truth that by firmness of purpose and by dulling one's talent for observation one can attain a uniformity which has a far more anesthetizing effect than the most capricious diversions, and which with time becomes stronger and stronger, like a formula of incantation. In excavating Herculaneum and Pompeii they found everything in place, just as the respective owners had left it. If I had lived in those days, the antiquarians would perhaps have encountered with amazement a man who walked with measured tread back and forth across the floor. In order to maintain this established and unchangeable order, I employed every means, I even went at certain times like the Emperor Domitian through the apartment with a flyswatter, pursuing every revolutionary fly. On the other hand, I preserved three or more flies which at definite times buzzed in the center of the room. Thus I lived, forgetting the world, as I thought, and by the world forgotten,[43] when one day I received a letter from my young friend. This was followed by more, always with an interval of about a month, though the letters furnished no indication from which

I could infer the distance of his place of abode. He himself does not wish to clarify anything, and it might well be a mystification he cautiously calculated by allowing the intervals between letters to vary from about five weeks to barely three. He "did not wish to put me to the trouble of carrying on a correspondence," and even if I were willing to answer his letter or at least send a reply, he does not wish to receive anything of the sort—he only desires to unburden himself.

I perceive from his letter (what I knew beforehand) that like every melancholy nature he is rather touchy; and in spite of his irritability, or rather because of it, he is in constant contradiction with himself. He wishes me to be his confidant, and yet he does not wish it, indeed it alarms him to reflect that I am; he feels safe with my so-called superiority, and yet it is disagreeable to him; he confides in me, and yet he desires no reply, indeed does not want to see me; he requires of me silence inviolable, "by all that is holy," and yet he is almost furious at the thought that I possess this power of keeping silent. The fact that I am his confidant no one must know, not a soul, hence he himself is unwilling to know it, and I must not know it. In order to explain this confusion to our mutual satisfaction and gratification he is so kind as to hint in a polite way that he really regards me as mentally deranged. How could I have courage to express any opinion about the audacity of this interpretation of my conduct? That in fact would be furnishing further proof of the correctness of the accusation, so it seems to me; whereas abstention from any reaction might well appear in his eyes a new indication of my ataraxia and weakness of mind, which is incapable of being affected by anything or of taking offense. So this is the thanks one gets for educating oneself daily and through a course of years to have only an ideal interest in people and to have this interest if possible in everyone in whom the idea is in motion! Lately I sought to be helpful to the idea in him, and now I reap the reward, namely, that I am to be and not to be both substantial existence and nothing, just as he pleases, and am not to enjoy the least recognition as being the former and so helping him again out of his self-contradiction. If he were to reflect how great an indirect recognition of me is implied in such a *Zumuthung*,[44] he presumably would again be furious. To be his confidant is more difficult than the most difficult of tasks, and he entirely forgets that by a single word, for example, by declining to receive his letters, I could mortify him very deeply. Not only was he punished who betrayed the Eleusinian Mysteries, but also the man who insulted this institution by not wanting to be initiated. The latter case, according to the report of a Greek writer, was that of Demonax,[45] who nevertheless got out of the scrape with a whole skin by his clever defense. My position as confidant is even more critical, for he has even more maidenly modesty with respect to his mysteries, he even gets angry when I do what he so insistently requires—when I keep silent.

If he thinks, however, that I have entirely forgotten him, he again does me injustice. Upon his sudden disappearance I really was afraid that he had laid violent hands upon himself. But such an occurrence does not usually remain hid for a long time, and therefore, since I neither heard nor read anything about it, I concluded that he must be alive, whereever he might be concealed. The girl whom he left in the lurch knew nothing whatever. One day he failed to put in an appearance and he let her hear nothing from him. Her transition to pain was not sudden; for it was only gradually the apprehensive presentiment dawned upon her, and only gradually did the pain become aware of itself, with the consequence that she slumbered gently into a dreamy obscurity as to what had occurred and what it might mean. For me the girl was new material for observation. My friend was not one of those who know how to torture everything out of the loved one and then cast her off. On the contrary, at the time of his disappearance she was in the best condition one could wish, in sound health, buxom, enriched by his whole poetical revenue, strongly nourished by the precious heart-stimulant of poetic illusion. It is seldom one finds a deserted maiden in this condition. When I saw her a few days after his disappearance she was still as nimble as a fish just caught. Generally such a girl is as starved as a fish in a well. I was convinced upon my word that he must be alive, and I was heartily glad to see that he had not grasped at the desperate expedient of giving himself out as dead. It is incredible how much confusion can come about in the domain of the erotic if one of the parties is pleased to want to die of sorrow, or to want to die so as to escape from the whole thing.[46] According to her own solemn declaration a girl would die of sorrow over the fact that her lover was a deceiver. But, behold, he was not a deceiver, and his intentions were perhaps better than she comprehended. What otherwise he might have done in the fullness of time, he could not now resolve to do, simply because she had allowed herself to make this asseveration, because, as he put it, she had employed an oratorical trick upon him, or in any case had said what a girl ought never to say, whether she believed he really was a deceiver (for then she ought to be too proud), or whether she still had faith in him (for then she ought to perceive that she is doing him a monstrous injustice). For a man to want to be dead in order to escape from the whole thing is the most wretched expedient that can be imagined and implies the most injurious offense against a girl. She believes he is dead, she wears mourning, she weeps and laments the deceased in all honesty. She must almost conceive disgust of her own feelings when later she discovers that he is alive and has not had the remotest thought of dying. Or if it is only in another life she first were to conceive a suspicion, not that he was actually dead (for that would then be incontrovertible), but that at the time in question he was dead, when he said he would die and when she sorrowed. Such a situation would be a theme for an apocalyptic writer[47] who had understood his Aristophanes (I mean in Greek, and I do not mean the simple men who are advanced to the doctorate like the *doctores cerei* of the Middle Ages) [48] and knew his Lucian. One might maintain the mistaken identity for a long time, for dead he was and dead he remained. The sorrowing girl would then awaken to begin where she left off, until she discovered that there was a little qualifying clause.[49]

Upon the reception of his letter, recollections were vividly revived in my soul, and it was by no means with cold indifference I followed the sequel of his story. When in the course of the letter I came to the not altogether inept declaration that I was mentally deranged, it at once occurred to me to exclaim, "Now he knows my most intimate secret, which is guarded by a jealousy with more than a hundred eyes." When I was personally in touch with him it did not escape my observation that with the utmost caution, before coming out with a word of confidence, he politely insinuated the remark that I was "queer." Well, that's what an observer must be prepared for. He must know how to give some sort of guarantee to the person who comes to confess. A girl in making her confession always requires a positive guarantee, a male requires a negative one. The reason for this is to be found in womanly devotion and humility, and in manly pride and self-sufficiency. What a comfort it is when the person from whom one seeks counsel and illumination is . . . mentally deranged! So one does not need to feel ashamed. To talk to such a person is in fact like talking . . . to a tree, "a thing one does simply for curiosity," as one can say if anyone were to inquire about it. An observer must know how to make himself light—otherwise no one will confide in him. Above all he must take care not to be ethically severe or to represent himself as the morally proper man. "He's a depraved man," one says, "he's been in the thick of it and had some mad adventures—*ergo* I can well confide in him, seeing that I am so much better." Well, that's all right for me; I demand nothing of men except the content of their conscious minds. That I weigh, and if it is heavy enough, no price is too high for me to pay.

Merely by reading the letter cursorily it became clear to me that his love affair had left a much deeper impression than I had conjectured. He must therefore have concealed from me some of his sentiments; and that is natural, for at that time I was only "queer," now I am "mentally deranged," and that is *etwas anders.* If that's how it stands, there is nothing left for him but to make a religious movement. So it is that love leads a person further and further on. What I so often have verified, I verify in this instance once again, that existence is after all infinitely profound, and its guiding power knows how to intrigue one better than all the poets rolled into one. In view of the disposition and the natural gifts of the young man I would have wagered that he would not be caught in love's net. For in this respect there are exceptions which cannot be declined in accordance with the case forms of the regular declensions. He had an unusually fine intelligence, distinguished especially by imagination. So soon as his creative activity was awakened he had enough to occupy him for his whole life, especially if he rightly understood himself and confined himself to the snug domestic delight of intellectual occupations and the enjoyment of imagination as a pastime, which is the most perfect surrogate for love, is far from entailing love's troubles and fatalities, and yet bears an express likeness to the most beautiful features of love's bliss. Such a nature has no need of woman-love—a situation which I am inclined to explain by the notion that in a previous existence he was a woman and retains a recollection of this now that he has become a man. Falling in love with a girl merely disturbs such a nature and is always a detriment to his task, for he almost is able to assume her rôle along with his own. This is disagreeable both to him and to her. Then on the other hand he has a very melancholy nature. As the first characteristic would restrain him from approaching any girl too nearly, so too would the second be his security if any cunning beauty should take it into her head to aspire after him. A profound melancholy in the sympathetic style is and will always be a complete humiliation to all feminine art. If a girl were to succeed in drawing him to her—the very instant she was prematurely exulting over her triumph it would occur to him to say to himself, "Art thou not committing a sin and an injustice against her in abandoning thyself to these sentiments? Wilt thou not be merely a stumbling-block to her?"—and then good night to all feminine intrigues. Now the situation is altered in a strange way; he has gone over to her side; he would be only too willing to perceive all the excellent qualities she possesses, would know how to present them better perhaps than she could, and to admire them more than she perhaps demands—but further than that she will never get him to go.

I had never expected that he might be permanently caught in a love affair. Yet existence is cunning. What makes him a captive is not the loveliness of the girl but regret that he has done her a wrong by upsetting her life. He had approached her ill-advisedly, he convinces himself that love cannot attain its realization in marriage, he can be happy without her (to the extent that he is able to be happy), especially with this new perquisite, a literary talent—so he breaks off; but now he cannot forget that he has done a wrong—just as if it were a wrong to break off when something cannot be carried through. In case he was unbiased, and in case it was said, "Here is the girl. Wilt thou approach her? Wilt thou fall in love?" it is pretty certain that he would say, "Not for the whole world. I once learned what comes of it. Such a thing one never forgets." And so indeed it is the question ought to be put, if he would not deceive himself. For him it is still a sure thing that the realization of his love is impossible. So he has come to the borders of the marvellous, and if after all this it is to come about, it must come about by virtue of the absurd. Does he not reflect at all upon the difficulties? Or with his clever pate is he perhaps only too prolific in inventions? Does he really love the girl? Or here again is she only the occasion which prompts him? Again it indubitably is not possession in the strictest sense which concerns him, or the content which develops from this situation; what concerns him is *return,* conceived in a purely formal sense. Though she were to die the day after, it would not any more disturb him, he would not feel the loss, for his nature would be at rest. The discord into which he has been thrown by contact with her would be resolved by the fact that he had actually returned to her. So again the girl is not a reality but a reflection of the movements within him and their exciting cause. The girl has a prodigious importance, he actually will never be able to forget her, but what gives her importance is not herself but her relation to him. She is as it were the boundary of his being. But such a relation is not erotic. Religiously speaking, one might say that it was as if God himself employed this girl to capture him; and yet the girl herself is not a reality but is like the artificial flies one sleaves upon hooks. I am entirely convinced that he is not in the least acquainted with the girl, notwithstanding he has been engaged to her and since that time she has never been out of his thoughts. She is the girl—then a period. Whether, speaking more concretely, she is this or that, whether she is charming, lovable, faithful, the sacrificial love for which one ventures everything and sets heaven and earth in commotion—upon this he does not reflect. If one were to vouch for the joy and the bliss he might expect in a truly erotic relationship, he presumably would not have a word to say. What concerns him is attained the very instant it proves possible to redeem his honor and regain his pride. As though it were not a matter of honor to defy such childish apprehensions. He anticipates perhaps that his whole personality would be ruined; but that is nothing if only he can avenge himself as it were upon existence which has mocked him by making him guilty when he was innocent, by making his attachment to life at this point meaningless, so that he must put up with it that every real lover sees in him a deceiver. Would not that be a burden to bear! However, perhaps I do not entirely understand him, perhaps he is concealing something, perhaps he is truly in love after all. So likely the end of the story will be that he puts me to death in order to confide in me his most holy secret. One can see that the position of an observer is a dangerous one. Nevertheless I could wish, merely for the sake of my interest as a psychologist, I might get the girl out of the way for an instant, get him to believe she was married; I wager I should get a different explanation; for his sympathy is so melancholy that I believe he imagines for her sake he is in love with her.

The problem which baffles him is neither more nor less than repetition. He is quite justified in not seeking light upon this problem either from modern philosophy or from the Greek; for the Greeks perform the opposite movement, and in this case a Greek would prefer to recollect, unless his conscience were to frighten him, and modern philosophy makes no movement, generally it only makes a fuss,[50] and what movement it makes is always within immanence, whereas repetition is always a transcendence. It is lucky that the young man does not seek any enlightenment from me, for I have abandoned my theory, I am adrift. Repetition is too transcendent for me also. I can circumnavigate myself, but I cannot erect myself above myself, I cannot find the Archimedean point. It is fortunate then that my friend is not seeking enlightenment from any world-renowned philosopher or from any *professor publicus ordinarius*; he has recourse to an unofficial thinker, a private practitioner, who once was in possession of worldly grandeur but now has retired from public life—in other words, he takes refuge in Job, who does not cut a figure in a university chair and with reassuring gestures vouch for the truth of this thesis, but who sits among the ashes and scrapes himself with a potsherd, and without interrupting this manual labor lets fall casual hints and remarks. Here he thinks he has found what he sought, and in this little circle of Job and the wife along with three friends the truth, as he thinks, seems more glorious and joyful and true than in a Greek symposium.

Even if he still were to desire my guidance, he would be seeking in vain. A religious movement I am unable to make, it is contrary to my nature. I am not inclined for this reason to deny the reality of such a thing, or to deny that one can learn a great deal from a young man. If he succeeds, he will have no admirer more zealous than I. If he succeeds, he will then be freed from all the touchiness he now shows in his relation to me. Only I cannot deny that the more I think about the case the more misgiving I feel about the girl. I suspect that in one way or another she has wished to make a captive of him by his melancholy. In that case I should not like to be in her place. It will come to a bad ending. Existence always avenges such behavior with the greatest severity.

August 15

MY SILENT CONFIDANT:

It will perhaps surprise you now to receive suddenly a letter from one who for you had long been dead and as good as forgotten, or forgotten and as good as dead. More than that feeling of surprise I dare not count upon. I picture to myself that the instant you receive this letter you will take out as it were the history of my case and say, "Just so, this was the man with the unhappy love affair. Where was it we left off? O yes, and these would naturally be the symptoms." Your calmness is really terrible! When I think of it my blood boils, and yet I am unable to break away; you enthrall me by a strange power. In talking with you I experience an indescribable sense of relief, for it is if one were talking with oneself or with an idea. But when one has talked oneself out and found solace in the outpouring . . . and then beholds your changeless expression and reflects that this is really a human being who stands there, a prodigiously shrewd man one has been talking to, then one becomes thoroughly alarmed. Good Lord! an afflicted man is always a bit jealous of his sorrow. It is not just in anybody he is willing to confide, he demands silence. One can be sure enough of that in your case. And yet when one has consoled oneself with this reflection one again becomes alarmed, for this silence of yours is as silent as the grave and presumably has in its keeping many similar depositions. You know all about everything, never get things mixed up, are able the next second to take out another secret and begin where you left off. Then one regrets having confided in you. Good Lord! an afflicted man is always a bit jealous of his sorrow. When he has initiated someone into the secret of his sorrow he wants to have that person feel the whole weight and importance of it. You do not disappoint this expectation, for you comprehend the finest nuance better than one does oneself. But the next instant I am in despair at the superiority you display in knowing everything and being unacquainted with nothing. If I were an autocratic ruler of all mankind, God help you! I would shut you up with me in a cage, so that you might belong to me alone, and then probably I would prepare for myself the most painful anguish by seeing you daily. You possess a demoniac power which is capable of tempting a man to be willing to venture everything, to want to have strength which ordinarily he does not possess, which ordinarily he does not desire to have, but only so long as you are looking at him, to want to seem to be what he is not, merely to purchase that approving smile which is an indescribable reward. I should like to see you the whole day and listen to you the whole night, and yet when it comes to acting I would not do it at any price in your presence. By one look you would confound everything. Face to face with you I have not the courage to admit my weakness; if once I had done that I should have been the most cowardly man alive, because it would seem to me then that I had lost everything. So you enthrall me by an indescribable power, and this same power alarms me. So I admire you, and yet at times it seems to me as if you were deranged. Or is it not a sort of mental derangement to have subjected every passion, every emotion of the heart, every feeling, to this cold disciple of reflection? Is it not mental derangement to be so normal, to be a mere idea, not a human being, not like the rest of us, pliant and yielding, capable of being lost and of losing ourselves? Is it not mental derangement to be always awake, always clearly conscious, never obscure and dreamy? At this instant I dare not see you, and yet I cannot do without you. Hence I am writing, and I beg you insistently not to put yourself to the trouble of sending me a reply. As a precaution this letter bears no address. This is my desire, and in this confidence it does me good to write to you, thus I am secure and happy with you.

Your plan was capital, indeed peerless. Even yet at certain moments I grasp like a child at the heroic shape you once held up to my admiring gaze with the declaration that it was my future destiny, the heroic shape which was to have made me a hero if I had had the strength to assume it. At that time it carried me away with all the power of illusion into a complete imaginative intoxication. Merely to think of cutting off the remainder of my life for the sake of one girl only! To make oneself a scoundrel, a deceiver, simply to show at how high a price one held her—for one does not sacrifice one's honor for a trifle! To brand myself, to throw away my life! To assume the rôle of vengeance and carry it out against myself, in a far more serious way than man's empty gossip can do it! Thus to be a hero, not in the eyes of the world, but within oneself, to have no plea to present before a human tribunal, but living immured within one's own personality to be one's own witness, one's own judge, one's own prosecutor, to be in oneself the one and only! To be exposed for the remainder of one's life to the thoughts which might well be the consequence of such a step, whereby, humanly speaking, one would in a way be giving up one's reason! To do all this for the sake of a girl! And if in this way the wrong might be redressed, then to have paid the girl, as you remarked, the most chivalrous and erotic compliment, surpassing every knightly exploit, even the most romantic, precisely for the fact that one did it all by oneself. This utterance of yours made a profound impression upon me. Of course it was not uttered with fanatical enthusiasm—imagine you fanatical! It was said with calm and cold common sense, with official knowledge, as if with a view to this case alone you had read through all the tales of knightly adventure. What it must be for a thinker to discover a new category, that it was for me to make a discovery in the domain of the erotic.

Unfortunately, however, I was not the artist capable of sustaining this role, nor had I the endurance for it. Fortunately I saw you only in remote places and rarely. If I could have had you by my side, if you could have been sitting in the room, even if it were in a corner, reading or writing, employed about irrelevant things, and yet, as I well know, alertly attentive to everything—in that case, I believe, I would have made a beginning at it. If I had done so, it would have been dreadful. Or is it not dreadful with cold composure, day after day, to bewitch the woman you love into a falsehood? And suppose she had grasped at expedients which were within her power—feminine adjurations! Suppose she had besought me with tears, adjured me by my honor, by my conscience, by my eternal salvation, my peace in life and in death, my peace here and hereafter! I shudder at the thought of it.[51]

I have not forgotten the particular suggestions you threw out, while I for the most part did not venture to oppose you and was only too much enchanted. You remarked that "in case a girl is justified in employing these expedients, one should let them have their due effect; what is more, one ought to assist her in employing them. One ought to be chivalrous enough toward a girl not only to be oneself but to be at the same time prosecutor on her side. If she is not justified, that is of no account, one is to let it slide off." That is true, absolutely and entirely true, but such good sense as this I do not possess. "What a foolish contradiction," you said, "one often meets with in men's cowardice and courage. A man is afraid of seeing the dreadful, but has courage to do it. You forsook the girl—that is the dreadful thing. You have courage for that, but to see her grow pale, to count her tears, to be witness to her distress, for this you have not courage. And yet in fact this is nothing in comparison with the other. If you know what you will, and why and how far, then you ought to behold it, ought to show respect for every argument, and not steal away from anything in the hope that your imagination is duller than reality. Thereby you deceive yourself also, for when the time comes your vivid imagination, being compelled to picture her distress, will erect itself more dreadfully than if you had seen it and had assisted her to make it as anguishing for you and as horrible as possible." That is true, every word is true, but it is a truth which might be true if the world were dead, so cold it is, so rigidly consistent. It does not convince me, it does not move me. I am weak, I admit; I was weak, I shall never become strong or intrepid. But take everything into consideration, put yourself in my place, and do not forget that you really love her as I loved her. I am convinced you would triumph, you would prevail, you would vanquish all horrors, you would befool her with your imposture. What would be the result? In case the most fortunate end did not come about, that the moment you were through with the exertion your hair became gray, and your soul an hour later had breathed its last—then, as your plan implied, this imposture must be continued. In that you would succeed, I am convinced. But are you not afraid of losing your mind? Are you not afraid of falling into that terrible passion they call contempt of mankind? To be so thoroughly in the right, to be faithful, and yet make oneself out to be a scoundrel, and then in one's deceit to scorn all the paltriness which often, I admit, puts on airs, but then along with that to mock also the better things in the world. What head could stand all this? Do you not believe it would often be necessary to get up at night and drink a glass of cold water or sit on the edge of the bed and think things over? Suppose I had begun it—it would have been impossible to persevere. I chose another expedient: left Copenhagen as quietly as possible and went to Stockholm. According to your plan this would have been incorrect. I ought to have gone openly. Imagine that she was standing on the dock. Imagine that my eye lit upon her only at the second when the machinery was set in motion! I believe I should have lost my mind. I do not doubt that you would have had strength to remain tranquil. If it had been necessary, and if you knew that she would appear on the dock, you would have taken the little seamstress with you and made the journey with her. If it had been necessary, you not only would have bribed a girl but (merely to be of service to the loved one) you would have seduced a girl, actually seduced her, lock, stock and barrel, if need were. But suppose you were suddenly to wake up in the night and not recognize yourself, were to confound yourself with that figure you used for your pious fraud. For I must admit that you certainly did not mean that one should begin such a thing light-mindedly; indeed you once let fall a word to the effect that this method never could be absolutely necessary unless the girl herself had been to blame, whether it was that she had been so thoughtless as not to take notice of a reminder of sympathy, or selfish enough to make no account of it.[52] But in this case precisely —would there not come an instant when she would understand what she ought to have done, and would be in despair at the consequences of leaving it undone—which consequences, however, were due not so much to her obduracy as to the whole personality of the other party? Would it not have been the case with her as it was with me? She would not have surmised, not have dreamt, what forces she was setting in motion, what passions she let loose, and then she would have been guilty of all and yet innocent. Would not this method be too severe for her? If in these circumstances I were to do anything, I should choose to scold, to become red in the face. But this silent objective condemnation!

No! No! No! I could not, I cannot, I will not—not for anything would I do it. No! No! No! I could fall into despair over these letters, which coldly and like idle loungers stand side by side, and the one "No" says no more than the other. You should hear the passion within me modulate them. Would that I stood beside you, and would that with my last "No" I could tear myself away from you, like Don Juan from the Commandant, whose hand was not colder than this sound common sense with which you irresistibly draw me to you. And yet if I were standing before you, I likely would hardly utter more than one "No," for before I got further you likely would burst out with the cold reply, "'Yes! yes!"

What I did was something very mediocre and bungling.

Well, you can smile at me. When a swimmer who is accustomed to spring from the ship's mast and to turn a somersault before reaching the water—when he challenges another to follow his example, and the other goes instead to the ship's ladder, sticks out one foot, then the other, and thereupon lets himself plump into the water—why, then he doesn't need to know how the first one did it. One day I failed to put in an appearance, and without having said a word to her I went aboard the steamboat for Stockholm. I fled away, concealing myself from everybody. God in heaven help her to find an explanation for herself! Have you seen her?—the girl I never mention by name, whose name I am not man enough to write, for my hand would shake with terror. Have you seen her? Is she pale, or perhaps dead, does she sorrow, has she forged an explanation which comforts her, is her gait still light, or is her head bowed and her figure despondent? Great God! my imagination can furnish me with everything. Are her lips blanched?—those lips which I admired, though I only took the liberty of kissing her hand. Is she moody and pensive who was as blissful as a child? Write me, I beseech you. No, do not write. I want no letter from you, nor to hear anything about her. I believe nothing, not a single soul, not even her. Though she stood before me bodily, though she were more cheerful than ever, I should not be joyful, I should not believe her, I should believe it was a deceit to mock me or to comfort me. Have you seen her? No! I hope you have not taken the liberty of seeing her or of intermeddling in my love affair. If I should get word of that! When a girl becomes unhappy there come at once all those hungry monsters who wish to sate their psychological hunger and thirst or to write novels. If I could only spring out and at least keep these blowflies away from the fruit which was sweeter to me than all else, the most delicate, smoother to look upon than a peach when in its happiest moment it adorns itself gloriously with silk and velvet.

What am I doing now? I begin all over again from the beginning, and then from the wrong end. I shun every outward reminder of the whole thing, yet my soul, day and night, waking and sleeping, is incessantly employed with it. Her name I never utter, and I give thanks to fate that through a misunderstanding I have acquired a false name. A name, my name—that properly belongs to her. Would that I might be rid of it. My own name is enough to remind me of everything, and the whole of existence, it seems to me, contains only allusions to this past. The day before my departure I read in the *Advertiser*,[53] "Sixteen yards of heavy black silk for sale on account of a change of purpose." What could have been the first purpose? Perhaps a bridal dress! What a pity I cannot offer in a newspaper my name for sale "on account of a change of purpose!" If a mighty spirit were to take away from me my name and were to offer it back glittering with immortal honors, I would cast it away, far away, and would ask like a beggar for the most insignificant name, the most meaningless, to be called No. 14 like the Blue Coat boys.[54] What good to me is a name which is not mine, what good a glorious name, though it were mine?

For what is the flattering voice of fame
Compared with love's sigh from a maiden's breast?[55]

What am I doing now? I go to sleep by day and lie awake at night. I am diligent and industrious, a model of domesticity and household thrift. I wet the finger, I tread the pedal, I stop the wheel, I set the spindle whirling—I spin. But when at night I have to put the spinning-wheel away . . . there was none—and where the yarn has gone no one knows but my cat. I am restless and nimble, but what comes of it all? He who tramples the peat accomplishes miracles compared with me. In short, if you wish to understand, if you wish to have a conception of my fruitless labour, then understand the poet's words spiritually, applying them to my thoughts—that is all I have to say:

Die Wolken treiben hin und her,
Sie sind so matt, sie sind so schwer;
Da stürzen rauschend sie herab,
Der Schoss der Erde wird ihr Grab.[56]

More I need not say to you, or better, I should rather have need of you in order to say more, in order to express what my fumbling thought can only crazily put together.

If I were to tell you everything in detail, my letter would be endlessly long, as long at least as a bad year, and as the times of which it is written, "I have no pleasure in them." I have, however, the advantage that I can break off anywhere, just as any instant I can cut the thread I myself am spinning.

And now, God keep you. The man who believes in existence is well insured, he will attain everything . . . just as surely as a man who to hide his feelings when he prays holds before his face a hat without a crown.

My dear Sir,
I have the honor, etc.
—yes, whether I will or no,
I nevertheless remain,

YOUR DEVOTED NAMELESS FRIEND.[57]

September 19

MY SILENT CONFIDANT:

Job! Job! Job! Job! Didst thou indeed utter nothing but these beautiful words, "The Lord gave, the Lord hath taken away, blessed be the name of the Lord"?[58] Didst thou say nothing more? In all thy distress didst thou merely continue to repeat these words? Why wast thou silent for seven days and nights? What went on in thy soul? When the whole world fell to pieces above thy head and lay in potsherds around thee, didst thou at once possess this superhuman composure, didst thou at once have love's interpretation and the frankheartedness of confidence and faith? Is thy door then closed against the afflicted man, can he expect from thee no other relief than that pitiable consolation which worldly wisdom offers by reciting a paragraph about the perfection of life? Hast thou nothing more to say? Dost thou not dare to say more than what the false comforters laconically mete out to the individual, what the false comforters, rigid as a master of ceremony, prescribe to the individual, that in the hour of distress it is seemly to say, "The Lord gave, the Lord hath taken away, blessed be the name of the Lord"—neither more nor less, just as one says "Prosit" when a person sneezes! No, thou who in the ripeness of thy days[59] wast a sword for the oppressed, a cudgel to protect the old, a staff for the decrepit, thou didst not fail men when all was riven asunder—then thou wast a mouth for the afflicted, and a cry for the contrite, and a shriek for the anguished, and an assuagement for all who were rendered dumb by torments, a faithful witness to the distress and grief a heart can harbor, a trustworthy advocate who dared to complain "in anguish of spirit"[60] and to contend with God. Why do people conceal this? Woe to him who devours the widow and the fatherless and defrauds them of their inheritance, but woe also to him who would slyly defraud the afflicted of the momentary consolation of relieving the oppression of his heart and "contending with God."[61] Or in our time is godly fear so great that the afflicted man does not need what was customary in those old days? Does one perhaps not dare to complain before God? Is it now godly fear that has become greater, or fear and cowardice? Nowadays people are of the opinion that the natural expression of sorrow, the desperate language of passion, must be left to poets, who as attorneys in a lower court plead the sufferer's cause before the tribunal of human compassion. Further than this no one ventures to go. Speak therefore, O Job of imperishable memory! Rehearse everything thou didst say, thou mighty advocate who dost confront the highest tribunal, no more daunted than a roaring lion! There is pith in thy speech, in thy heart there is godly fear, even when thou dost complain, when thou wouldst justify thy despair against thy friends who rise up like robbers to assault thee with their speeches, and even when incited by thy friends thou dost tread their wisdom under foot and despise their defense of the Lord, accounting it the finite shrewdness of a veteran courtier or a worldly-wise minister of state. Thee I have need of, a man who knows how to complain aloud, so that his complaint echoes in heaven where God confers with Satan in devising schemes against a man.[62]

Complain! The Lord is not afraid, he is well able to defend himself, but how might he be able to speak in his defense if no one ventures to complain as it is seemly for a man to do? Speak, lift up thy voice, speak aloud, God surely can speak louder, he possesses the thunder—but that too is an answer, an explanation, reliable, trustworthy, genuine, an answer from God himself, an answer which even if it crush a man is more glorious than gossip and rumor about the righteousness of providence which are invented by human wisdom and circulated by effeminate creatures and eunuchs.

My benefactor of imperishable memory, tormented Job,

dare I join myself to thy company, may I listen to thee? Do not repel me, I am not standing here as an impostor beside thy ash heap, my tears are not false, although all I am able to do is to weep with thee. The joyful man seeks the company of gladness, although what gladdens him most intimately is the joy which dwells within him; and so the afflicted man seeks the company of sorrow. I have not been in possession of the world, have not had seven sons and three daughters,[63] but he too may have lost all who possessed but little, he too may as it were have lost sons and daughters who lost his loved one, and he too was so to speak "smitten with sore boils" who has lost honor and pride, and along with that the will to live and the meaning of life.

YOUR

NAMELESS FRIEND.

October 11

MY SILENT CONFIDANT:

My life has been brought to an *impasse,* I loathe existence, it is without savor, lacking salt and sense. If I were hungrier than Pierrot, I should not be inclined to eat the explanation people offer. One sticks one's finger into the soil to tell by the smell in what land one is: I stick my finger into existence—it smells of nothing. Where am I? What is this thing called the world? What does this word mean? Who is it that has lured me into the thing, and now leaves me there? Who am I? How did I come into the world? Why was I not consulted, why not made acquainted with its manners and customs but was thrust into the ranks as though I had been bought of a "soul-seller"?[64] How did I obtain an interest in this big enterprise they call reality? Why should I have an interest in it? Is it not a voluntary concern? And if I am to be compelled to take part in it, where is the director? I should like to make a remark to him. Is there no director? Whither shall I turn with my complaint? Existence is surely a debate—may I beg that my view be taken into consideration? If one is to take the world as it is, would it not be better never to learn what it is? What is a deceiver? Does not Cicero say that a deceiver can be found out by asking the question *cui bono*?[65] I allow everyone to ask, and I ask everyone, whether I have had any profit by making myself and a girl unhappy. Guilt—what does that mean? Is it witchcraft? Is it not definitely known how a person becomes guilty? Will anybody respond? Is it not then of the utmost importance to the gentlemen involved in the thing?

My mind is at a standstill, or rather I am going out of it. One moment I am tired and weary, yes, dead for sheer indifference; at another moment I am frantic and travel bewildered from one end of the world to the other, to find one person upon whom I could expend my wrath. The whole content of my being shrieks in contradiction against itself. How did it come about that I became guilty? Or am I not guilty?[66] Why am I then so called in all human tongues? What a wretched invention human language is: it says one thing and means another!

Is it not something that has simply happened to me, is not the whole thing an accident? Could I know beforehand that my whole nature would undergo a change, that I should become another man? Did that perhaps break out which lay obscurely hidden in my soul? But if it lay there obscurely, how could I foresee it? But if I could not foresee it, then I am not guilty. If I had had an attack of apoplexy, would I then too have been guilty? What is the human speech they call language, what is it but a miserable jargon understood only by a clique? Are not the dumb beasts wiser for the fact that they never talk about such things?—Am I unfaithful? In case she were to continue to love me and would never love anyone else, she would be faithful to me. If I continue to wish to love her only, am I unfaithful? We both do in fact the same thing; how then do I become a deceiver if I show my faithfulness by deceiving? Why must she be in the right, and I in the wrong? If we both are true, why then is this expressed in human language by saying that she is faithful, and I a deceiver?

Though the whole world were to rise up against me, though all the scholastics were to dispute with me, though my life were at stake, I nevertheless maintain that I am in the right. No one shall wrest this conviction from me, though there is no language in which I can give utterance to it. I have acted correctly. My love cannot express itself in a marriage. If I were to marry her, she would be crushed. Perhaps the possibility of marriage appeared alluring to her. I cannot help that—so it was to me. The very instant reality comes into question, all is lost, it is then too late. The reality in which she is to find her significance is for me only a shadow which runs alongside of my proper spiritual reality, a shadow which at one moment would make me laugh, at another would intrude disturbingly in my existence. It would end in my wanting to touch her, fumblingly, as if I were grasping a shadow, or stretching out my hand after a shadow. Would not her life be ruined? Indeed she is as if dead to me, yea, she might awaken in my soul the temptation to wish her dead. In case I were to crush her, she would be volatilized precisely at the instant I would make her a reality—whereas in the other case I retain her as a genuine reality, though in a sense it is a reality full of dread. What then? Why, then language says that I am guilty, for I ought to have foreseen this.—What sort of power is this which would take from me my honor and my pride, and would do it in such a senseless way? Am I then a victim of fate? Must I then be guilty and be a deceiver, whatever I do, even if I do nothing?—Or am I crazy? Then the best thing would be to shut me up; for human cowardice is especially afraid of the pronouncements of crazy people and of the dying. Crazy—what does it mean? What am I to do in order to enjoy public esteem and to be regarded as wise? Why no answer? I offer a reasonable *douceur* to anybody who invents a new word. I have stated the alternatives. Is anybody so wise that he knows more than two? But if he knows more, then it is nonsense that I am crazy, unfaithful, and a deceiver, whereas the girl is faithful, sane, and esteemed by everybody. Or is it to be laid to my charge that I made the first period of our relationship so beautiful? Thanks for the compliment! When I saw her joy in being loved, I put myself and everything she pointed to under the magic power of love's enchantment. Is it a fault that I could do this or that I did it? Who is at fault that I could do this or that I did it? Who is at fault in this, unless it be the girl herself and the third party whom no one knows, from whence it came that I was touched with the stroke of a wand and transformed? What I have done they praise in others.—Or is it my compensation that I became a poet? I decline any compensation, I demand my rights, i.e. my honor. I have not prayed to become a poet, and I would not buy the gift at that price.—Or, if I am guilty, then surely I must be able to repent of my guilt and make amends. Tell me how. Should I perhaps repent furthermore of the fact that the world takes the liberty of playing with me like a child with a June bug?—Or is it best to forget the whole thing? Forget! I have ceased to be if I forget this. Or what a life it would be if along with the loved one I have lost honor and pride—and lost them in such a way that no one knows how this thing came about for which I can make no reparation! Shall I let myself then be pushed out? But why was I then pushed in? I didn't demand it.

He who is put on bread and water is better off than I. My reflections are, humanly speaking, the scantiest diet imaginable; and yet, in spite of my microcosmic proportions, I experience a satisfaction in comporting myself as macrocosmically as possible.

I do not talk to anybody; and yet, not to break off all communication with men, or to give them fudge for their money, I have made a considerable collection of poems, pithy sayings, proverbs, and brief extracts from the immortal Greek and Latin writers who in all ages have been admired. To this anthology I have added several capital quotations from Balle's Lesson Book,[67] published under the auspices of the Orphan Asylum. So if anybody puts a question to me, I have the answer ready. I can quote the Classics just as well as Peer Deacon[68] could, and in addition to that I can quote Balle's Lesson Book. "Even though we have attained all the honor one could desire, we ought not to let ourselves be carried away into pride and arrogance." I do not deceive anyone. How many people are there after all who speak a truth or make a good remark? "Under the word 'world' is comprehensively included heaven and earth and all that in them is."

What good would it do if I were to say something? There

is no one who would understand me. My pain and my suffering are nameless, as I myself am—I who, though I have no name, nevertheless remain perhaps something to you, and in any case remain

Devotedly yours.

November 15

MY SILENT CONFIDANT:

If I had not Job! It is impossible to describe and to *nuancer* what significance he has for me, and how manifold his significance is. I do not read him as one reads another book with the eye, but I read this book as it were with my heart, with the eye of the heart I read it, understanding as in a state of *clairvoyance* every particular passage in the most various ways. As the child puts his school-book under the pillow to make sure that he shall not have forgotten his lesson when he wakes up in the morning, so do I take the book with me to bed at night. Every word of his is food and clothing and medicine for my ailing soul. Now one word rouses me from my lethargy, so that I awaken to new disquietude; now it quiets the fruitless fury within me and puts an end to the horrible feeling of mute nausea produced by passion. You surely have read Job? Read him, read him over and over again. I cannot bring myself to quote a single outburst of his in a letter to you, although it is my joy to make transcripts again and again of all that he said, now in Danish characters, now in Latin script, now on a sheet of one size, now on that of another size. Every one of these transcripts is laid like a so-called "God's-hand-poultice"[69] upon my sick heart. And upon whom indeed was God's hand laid as it was upon Job! But quote him—that I cannot do. That would be to wish to give his words my flavoring, to want to make his word mine in the presence of another man. When I am alone I do that, I appropriate every word; but so soon as anyone is present I know well what a young man has to do when old folks talk.

In the whole Old Testament there is no figure one approaches with so much confidence and frank-heartedness and trustfulness as Job, just because everything about him is so human, because he lies upon the confines of poetry. Nowhere in the world has the passion of pain found such an expression. What is Philoctetus[70] with his complaints, which constantly remain on the earth and do not terrify the gods! What is his situation compared with that of Job, where the idea is always in movement!

Forgive me for telling you everything. You are my confidant, and you are not able to reply. If anyone were to get to know this, it would distress me indescribably. At night I leave all the candles in my room lit, illuminating the whole apartment. Then I arise and read in a loud voice, almost shouting, one passage or another from Job. Or I open my window and shout out his words into the world. If Job is merely a poetical figure, if there never was any man who talked like this, then I make his words mine and assume the responsibility. More I cannot do, for who has such eloquence as Job, or is capable of improving anything that he said?

Although I have read the book again and again, every word is new to me. When I come across a word it is at that instant born, primitively, or makes a primitive impression upon my soul. Like a drunkard I imbibe little by little all the intoxication of passion, until with these slow sippings I become almost dead-drunk. On the other hand, I hasten toward the book with indescribable impatience. A half word, and with that my soul plunges into his thought and into his outbursts. More swiftly than the plummet seeks the bottom of the sea, more swiftly than the lightning seeks the conductor, my soul slips into his thought and there remains.

At other times I am quieter. Then I do not read, I sit shrunken together like an ancient ruin and gaze at everything. Then it seems to be as though I were a little child who goes pottering about the room or sits in a corner with his toys. I have a strange sensation. I cannot understand what it is that makes the grown folks so passionate, I cannot understand what they are quarrelling about, and yet I cannot help listening. Then it seems to me that it was bad people gave Job all that affliction, that it was his friends who now sit and bark at him. Then I weep loudly, a nameless dread of the world and of life and of men and of everything wrings my heart.

Then I awake and begin again to read him aloud with all my might and with all my heart. Then suddenly I am struck dumb, I hear nothing more, see nothing, only in obscure outlines have I a presentiment of Job sitting upon his ash heap, and of his friends; but no one says a word,[71] but this silence conceals within itself all that is horrible, as a secret which no one dare mention.

Then the silence is broken, and Job's tormented soul bursts out in a mighty shout. Him I understand, these words I make my own. The same instant I sense the contradiction in this, and then I smile at myself as one smiles at a little child who has put on his father's clothes. Or is it not something to smile at if anyone else but Job were to say,[72] "O that a man might go to law with God, like a son of man with his fellow!" And yet dread comes over me as if I did not yet understand it, but as though I should some day come to understand, as though the terror about which I read was already lurking for me as I read about it, just as one becomes ill of the disease one reads about.

December 14

MY SILENT CONFIDANT:

Everything has its time, the frenzy of the fever is past, I am like a convalescent. The secret in Job, the vital power, the nerve, the idea, is that in spite of everything Job is in the right. By this claim he constituted himself an exception to all human juridical interpretations, while by his tenacity of purpose and by his power he demonstrated his authority, his well warranted authority. For him every human explanation is only a misunderstanding, and in relation to God all his affliction is only a sophism, which he indeed cannot resolve, but which he trusts God can resolve. Every *argumentum ad hominem* is used against him, but he buoyantly maintains his conviction. He claims to be on good terms with God, he knows that he is innocent and pure in his inmost heart, where he is conscious that God knows it too, and yet the whole of existence contradicts him. The greatness of Job consists in the fact that the passion of freedom within him is not stifled or tranquilized by a false expression. Under similar circumstances this passion is often stifled in a man for the fact that pusillanimity and paltry dread had made him believe that he suffered for the sake of his sins, when such was not the case at all. The soul of such a man lacked persistence in carrying a thought through when the world persisted in thinking the contrary. When a man thinks that a misfortune overtook him because of his sins, that may be pretty and genuine and humble, but it may also be because he obscurely conceives of God as a tyrant, a notion to which a man at the same instant gives a meaningless expression by subsuming God under ethical categories.—Nor did Job become demoniac. Thus, for example, a man may acknowledge that God is in the right, notwithstanding he believes that he himself is. He desires to show in a way that he loves God, even when God would tempt the man that loves him. Or he says that God cannot alter the world for his sake, and so he will be magnanimous enough to continue to love God. This is a thoroughly demoniac person which deserves a separate psychological treatment. It sometimes puts an end to what we may call the quarrel in a humorous spirit, rather than make too much fuss; or it culminates in an egotistic and defiant reliance upon the strength of its own feeling.

Job continues to uphold the claim that he is in the right. He does this in such a way that he testifies thereby to the noble human dauntlessness which knows what a man is, that he is frail as the life of a flower and soon fades, but that nevertheless in the possession of freedom he is great, and has a consciousness of his freedom which God himself cannot take away from him, though it was he that gave it. Job also maintains his claim in such a way that one can see in him the love and trustfulness which is assured that God can explain everything, if only one can get him to speak.

The friends provide Job with plenty to do; the dispute with them is a purgatory in which the thought that he is nevertheless right becomes purified. If he himself had lacked power and inventiveness to alarm his conscience and dismay his soul, had lacked imagination to make him fearful for himself on account of the fault or guilt which secretly he might harbor in his inmost heart, then the friends would have helped him by their broad hints and by their impudent accusations, which like envious dousing-rods might be expected to summon forth what lay most deeply concealed. His misfortune is their principal argument, and thus everything is established to their satisfaction. One might suppose that Job would either lose his mind or collapse out of sheer weariness with his misery, surrendering unconditionally. Eliphaz, Bildad, Zophar, and above all Elihu who rises to his feet *integer* when the others are weary, play variations upon the theme that his misfortune is a chastisement; he is to repent, pray for forgiveness, then all will be well again.

Job, however, maintains his contention. His claim is like a passport with which he takes leave of the world and mankind, it is a demand which men protest, but Job has no mind to rescind it. He employs every expedient to move the hearts of his friends. He tries to move them to compassion ("Have pity upon me"),[73] he terrifies them by his voice ("Ye are forgers of lies").[74] In vain. The cry of his pain becomes more and more vehement; with the increasing opposition of the friends his reflection becomes absorbed in his sufferings. Yet this does not move the friends, this is not the question at issue. They would willingly agree with him that he suffers and that he has reason to cry aloud, that "the wild ass does not bray when it has grass,"[75] but they require him to perceive chastisement in his sufferings.

How then does one explain Job's claim? The explanation is this, that the whole thing is a *trial of probation.* This explanation, however, suggests new and unresolved difficulties, which I have endeavored to make clear to myself in the following way. Science does indeed deal with and explain existence, including man's relation to God. But what science is there of such a sort that it has place for a relationship defined as probation, which when conceived in the light of the infinite does not exist, but exists only for the individual? Such a science there is not, and there cannot possibly be. Moreover: how does the individual get to know that it is a trial of probation? The individual who has any conception whatever of an existence in thought and a being of consciousness readily perceives that this is not so quickly done as said, nor so quickly over as it is said, nor so quickly grasped as it is said. First the occurrence in question must be clarified by abstracting it from the cosmic connection and receive a religious baptism and a religious name; then one has to present oneself for inspection before the tribunal of ethics, and then comes the expression, "trial." Before this moment the individual did not exist by virtue of thought. Every explanation was still possible, and the whirlpool of passion was let loose. Only the men who have no conception or an unworthy conception of living by virtue of spirit are in this respect quickly done with it; they have a half hour's reading with which to console men, just as not a few philosophical apprentices have a hasty result to offer.

The greatness of Job does not therefore consist solely in the fact that he said, "The Lord gave, the Lord hath taken away, blessed be the name of the Lord"—which he uttered, moreover, at the beginning and did not repeat later. But Job's significance is that the border conflicts incident to faith are fought out in him, and that the prodigious insurrection of the wild and bellicose powers of passion are here set forth.

Therefore Job does not tranquilize like a hero of faith, but he provides temporary relief. Job represents as it were the whole weighty plea presented on man's behalf in the great suit between God and man, the prolix and dreadful process of justice which had its ground in the fact that Satan raised a suspicion against Job, and which ends with the explanation that the whole thing is a trial of probation.

This category, "trial of probation," is neither aesthetic, nor ethical, nor dogmatic, it is entirely transcendent. Not until it is known to be a trial could a place be found for it in a dogmatic work. But so soon as this knowledge is at hand the elasticity of trial is weakened, and the category is really a different one. This category is absolutely transcendent and places man in a purely personal relationship of contradiction to God, in such a relationship that he cannot rest content with any explanation at second hand.

The fact that a great many people have this category ready at once on every occasion, the gruel needing only to be heated, merely proves that they have not comprehended it. The man who has a well developed consciousness of the world has a very long detour to make before he reaches this category. Such was the case with Job, who proves the breadth of his conception of the world by the firmness with which he is able to eschew all crafty ethical evasions and cunning wiles. Job is not a hero of faith, he gives birth with prodigious pains to the category of "trial"—precisely because he is so developed that he does not possess this category in childish immediacy.

I can see well that this category might have a tendency to erase and suspend reality as a whole by defining it as a trial with relation to eternity. Yet this objection has no force for me; for since a trial is *temporary* it is *eo ipso* qualified by relation to time and must be done away with in time.

So much I am able to perceive now, and as I have taken the liberty of initiating you into it all, I write these last lines personally to you. From you, as you know, I require nothing —except that I may take the liberty of remaining

Devotedly yours.

January 13

MY SILENT CONFIDANT:

The tempests have raged themselves out—the thunderstorm is past—Job has been reproved before the eyes of men—the Lord and Job understand one another, they are reconciled, "the intimacy of the Lord dwells again in the tents of Job as in the former days"[76]—men have learnt to understand Job, they come now to eat bread with him,[77] to bemoan and comfort him, his brothers and sisters make each of them a present to him of a piece of money and a gold ring—Job is blessed and has received everything *double*. This is what is called a *repetition*. How much good a thunderstorm does after all! How blessed it must be after all to be reproved of God! Ordinarily a man is so likely to harden himself against reproof; when God passes judgment a man loses himself and forgets the pain in the love which is intent upon educating.

Who could have conceived this conclusion? And yet no other conclusion is conceivable—and neither is this. When everything has come to a standstill, when thought is brought to a halt, when speech becomes mute, when the explanation in bewilderment seeks the way home—then there must be a thunderstorm. Who can understand this? And yet who can find out any other conclusion?

Did Job lose his case? Yes, eternally; for he can appeal to no higher court than that which judged him. Did Job gain his case? Yes, eternally . . . for the fact that he lost his case *before God*.[78]

So then there is such a thing as a repetition. When does it come about? Well, that's not so easy to say in any human language. When did it come about for Job? When all *conceivable* human certitude and probability pronounced it impossible. Little by little he loses everything; therewith hope vanishes gradually in proportion as reality, far from being mollified, makes heavier and heavier claims upon him. In the sense of immediacy all is lost. His friends, especially Bildad,[79] know of only one way out, that by submitting to his chastisement he might hope to have a repetition in superabundance. For that Job is not willing. Thereupon the plot thickens, so that only by a thunderstorm can it be resolved.

For me this narrative contains an indescribable consolation. Was it not lucky I did not follow your much admired plan so shrewdly thought out? Perhaps, humanly speaking, it was cowardice on my part, but perhaps now divine governance can the more readily come to my aid.

There is only one thing I regret, namely, that I did not beg the girl to give me my liberty. I an convinced she would have done it. For who indeed can conceive of a girl's magnanimity?[80] And yet I cannot altogether regret it, for I know that I abstained from doing it because I was too proud for her sake to do it.

In case I had not Job! I say no more for fear of burdening you with my perpetual refrain.

Devotedly yours.

February 17

MY SILENT CONFIDANT:

Here I sit. On the plea of "innocent" (as they say in thieves' Latin), or "by the King's grace"?[81] I don't know. I know only this, that I am sitting and that I have not budged from the spot. Here I stay—whether on my head or on my heels I do not know; I know only this, that here I stay and that for a whole month I have remained *suspenso gradu* without drawing my foot toward me or making the least movement.

I am expecting a thunderstorm . . . and repetition. Yet—if only the thunderstorm were to come! At the very thought I am joyful, indescribably blissful—even if my sentence were to be that no repetition is possible.

What is this thunderstorm to accomplish? It is to make me capable of being a husband. That will crush my whole personality—I am ready for it. It will make me unrecognizable in my own eyes—I do not waver, although I am standing upon one leg. My honor is saved, my pride is redeemed; and, however it may transform me, I hope nevertheless that the recollection will remain with me as an inexhaustible comfort, will remain when that has come to pass which in a certain sense I fear more than self-slaughter, because it will disturb me on an entirely different scale. If the thunderstorm does not come, then I shall resort to cunning; then I shall not die by any means, but make out that I am dead, so that kindred and friends might bury me. When they lay me in the coffin I shall very quietly pocket my expectation. Nobody will get to know it, for otherwise they would beware of burying a man who still had life in him.

For the rest, I am doing everything in my power to make a husband out of myself. I sit and trim myself, removing everything incommensurable, in order to become commensurable. Every morning I lay aside all the impatience and infinite striving of my soul—to no avail, the next instant it is there again. Every morning I shave off the beard in which I laugh[82]—to no avail, next morning my beard is as long as ever. I revoke myself, as a bank recalls its notes in order to put new ones in circulation—that will not succeed. I dispose of all my idea-wealth, my stocks and bonds, to buy matrimonial pocket-money—alas, in that coinage my riches come to very little.

However, I will be brief; my attitude and my situation do not allow me to employ many words.

Devotedly yours.[83]

NOTWITHSTANDING I retired from the world long ago and renounced all theorizing, I cannot deny that the young man, because of my interest in him, put me a bit out of my pendulum-regularity. This much is easily clear to me from his last letter, that he is laboring under a complete misapprehension. What he is suffering from is a misapplied melancholy magnanimity for which there is properly no place but in a poet's brain. He expects a thunderstorm which is to make him over into a husband—perhaps he means a nervous apoplexy. The reality is exactly the opposite. He is the sort of man that says, "Whole battalion right-about face," instead of facing right-about himself[84] which can be expressed in another way: the girl must be got out of the way. If I were not so old, I might ask to have the pleasure of taking her myself, just to help the man.

He rejoices that he has not followed my "shrewd" plan. That's exactly like him. To think that even at this moment he cannot perceive that it would have been the only correct plan! One can't have any dealings with him and it is lucky he doesn't want a reply, for it would be ridiculous to carry on a correspondence with a man who holds in his hand such a trump as a thunderstorm. If only he possessed my shrewdness! Whether, when that event he is counting upon has come about, he would want to give it a religious expression—that's his affair, I have no objection. But it is always well to have done everything human shrewdness can prescribe. I ought to have been in his place, I should have been of more help to the girl. Now she will perhaps find it more difficult to forget him. She did not get to the point of screaming, and that is a misfortune. There must be some crying out, that is a good thing, just as it is a good thing when blood comes with a bruise. One must let a girl cry, and then afterwards she has nothing to cry for, but quickly forgets.

He did not follow my advice, and now she presumably sits and grieves. I can well perceive that this must be exceedingly disastrous for him. In case there was a girl who was inclined to sit and grieve for me in this fashion, I should fear her more than anything in the world, more than a democrat fears a tyrant. She would disturb me profoundly, I should be conscious of her every instant, as one is of a sore tooth. She would disturb me because she was ideal, and I, when it comes to that, am too proud of my sensibility to tolerate the notion that anybody in the world has a stronger or more lasting sentiment than I. If she were to remain upon that ideal pinnacle, I might have to put up with it that my life, instead of progressing, remained stationary, *in pausa*. Perhaps there might be some man who was unable to bear the painful admiration she compelled him to feel for her, and would become so envious that he would resort to every expedient to destroy her—poison, for example.

For though she were to say, as so often has been said and written and printed and read and forgotten and repeated, "I have *loved* thee—now I admit it" (saying "now" in spite of the fact that she presumably had said it hundreds of times before); "I have loved thee more dearly than God" (which is not saying little . . . and yet not saying much in our godfearing times when godly fear is so rare a phenomenon)—that would not disturb the man. The ideal is not to die of sorrow, but to keep well and cheerful if possible, and yet rescue one's sentiment. To take another man is no great exploit. That is a weakness, a very simple and plebeian virtuosity in honor of which only the town militia would present arms. Everyone who has an artistic eye for life can readily see that this is a blunder, which cannot be repaired even by marrying seven times.

Moreover, when he regrets that he had not begged her to give him his freedom, he needn't put himself out, that wouldn't have helped much, in all human probability he would have furnished her arms against himself, for to beg for one's freedom is really something quite different from supplying a girl with the explanation that she is one's muse. Here one perceives again that he is a poet. A poet is as it were born to be a dupe of the girls. Though the girl had made a fool of him right before his open eyes, he would have thought it magnanimity on her part. He may rather congratulate himself that he did not commit this imprudence. She then presumably would have gone to work in dead earnest. She would have tried her hand not merely on the little multiplication table of the erotic (which is lawful, and which she has a right to do), but also at the big table of marriage which deals with greater magnitudes. She would have taken God as her sponsor, invoked everything that is holy, laid under embargo every precious memory which might dwell in his soul.[85] In this field, when opportunity offers, many young girls employ without any embarrassment a falsehood which not even a seducer would permit himself to employ. One who in the erotic field operates "by God's help," and wants to be loved "for God's sake," ceases to be oneself and becomes stronger than heaven and more important than a man's eternal blessedness. Suppose the girl had schooled him in that fashion, he perhaps would never have forgotten it, never got over it, since presumably he would have been too chivalric to listen to a sensible word from me, but would have let every outburst of hers count as genuine coin to be preserved as eternal truth. Suppose that afterwards this was shown to be an exaggeration, a little lyrical impromptu, a sentimental diversion.—O well, his magnanimity idea would perhaps have helped him in this case also.

My friend is a poet, and to a poet belongs essentially this fanatical faith in woman. I, if I may say it with all due respect, am a prosaist. So far as the other sex is concerned, I have my own opinion, or rather I have none at all, since I have very seldom seen a girl whose life could be construed in terms of a category. Generally a woman lacks the logical consistency which is necessary if one is to hold a human being in admiration or in contempt. She deceives herself before she deceives another, and therefore one has no scale to judge her by.

My young friend had better look out. I have not much confidence in his thunderstorm. I believe he would have done well to follow my advice. The idea was in movement in the young man's love, and for that reason I was interested in him. The plan I proposed applied the idea as a measuring rod. That is the surest scale in the world. When a man watches that attentively, everybody who would deceive him is fooled. The idea was applied—that I thought he owed to the loved one and to himself. If she had been capable of living in that fashion (which requires no extraordinary talents but only sincerity), then the moment he left her she would have said to herself, "I now have nothing more to do with him, whether he was a deceiver or not, whether he returns or not; what I retain is the ideality of my own love, and that I shall know how to hold in honor," If she had done this, then my friend's situation would have been painful enough, for then he would have remained in sympathetic grief and distress. However, who would not put up with that when in the midst of all his sorrow he had the joy of admiring the loved one? His life would have been arrested like hers, but it would have been arrested as a river is arrested in its course when it is enchanted by the spell of music.—If she were not capable of using the idea as the regulative principle of her life, then he might properly reflect that he had not troubled her life by showing his pain.

May 31

MY SILENT CONFIDANT:

She is married—to whom I do not know, for when I read it in the paper it was as though I had a touch of apoplexy, and I lost the notice and have not had patience to make a closer inspection. I am again myself, here I have the repetition, I understand everything, and existence seems to me more beautiful than ever. It came as a thunderstorm after all, though I owe its occurrence to her magnanimity. Whomever she has chosen (I will not even say "preferred," for as a husband every man is preferable to me), she has at any rate showed magnanimity toward me. Though he were the most beautiful man in the world, a paragon of amiability, capable of enchanting every girl, and though she may have brought the whole sex to despair by giving him her "Yes," she nevertheless has acted magnanimously toward me—if in no other respect, at least by forgetting me completely. What is so beautiful as feminine magnanimity! Let the earthly queen of beauty fade, let the luster of her eyes be dimmed, let her erect figure be bent by the weight of years, let her curls lose their fascinating power when they are hidden by the humble coif, let her royal glance which swayed the world now embrace and watch over with motherly love the family circle she protects—a girl who has been so magnanimous never grows old. Let existence reward her as it has, let it give her what she loved more—it gave me also what I loved more . . . myself, and gave it through her magnanimity.

I am again myself. This self which another would not pick up from the road I possess again. The discord in my nature is resolved, I am again unified. The terrors which found support and nourishment in my pride no longer enter in to distract and separate.

Is there not then a repetition? Did I not get everything doubly restored? Did I not get myself again, precisely in such a way that I must doubly feel its significance? And what is a repetition of earthly goods which are of no consequence to the spirit—what are they in comparison with such a repetition? Only his children Job did not receive again double,[86] because a human life is not a thing that can be duplicated. In that case only spiritual repetition is possible, although in the temporal life it is never so perfect as in eternity, which is the true repetition.

I am again myself, the machinery has been set in motion. The snares in which I was entangled have been hewn asunder, the magic spell which bewitched me so that I could not return to myself has now been broken. There is no one any more who lifts up her hands against me, my liberation is assured, I am born to myself, for so long as Ilithia[87] folds her hands one who is in travail cannot bring to birth.

It is over, my yawl is afloat, the next minute I am where my soul's yearning was, where the ideas foam with elemental rage, where thoughts arise boisterously like the nations in migration, where at another season there is a stillness like the profound silence of the South Sea, so that one can hear oneself speak even though the movement goes on in one's own interior—there where one every instant stakes one's life, every instant loses it, and wins it again.

I belong to the idea. When that beckons me I follow, when it appoints a tryst I await it day and night, no one calls me at midday, no one awaits me at supper. When the idea calls I forsake everything, or rather I have nothing to forsake, I deceive nobody, I grieve nobody by being faithful to the idea, my spirit is not grieved by having to grieve another. When I return home no one reads in my looks, no one deciphers in my countenance, no one extorts from my being an explanation which not even I can give to another, as to whether I am blissful in gladness or despondent in distress, as to whether I have gained life or have lost it.

The chalice of inebriation is again held out to me, already I inhale its fragrance, already I am sensible of its foaming music—but first a libation to her who saved a soul which sat in the solitude of despair. Hail to feminine magnanimity! Long life to the high flight of thought, to moral danger in the service of the idea! Hail to the danger of battle! Hail to the solemn exultation of victory! Hail to the dance in the vortex of the infinite! Hail to the breaking wave which covers me in the abyss! Hail to the breaking wave which hurls me up above the stars!

To

N__________ N__________, Esq.

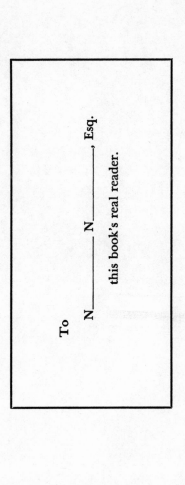

this book's real reader.

Copenhagen, August[88] *1843*

MY DEAR READER:

Forgive me for talking to thee so intimately—but are we not *unter uns*? For though thou be a fictitious figure, thou art surely not a plurality but only one, so that after all we are just thou and I.

If it is taken for granted that everyone is a reader in an unreal sense who reads a book for this or that casual reason having nothing to do with the book, then there would not be many real readers left, even for the authors whose clientele is very numerous. For who in our time would waste an instant upon the whimsical thought that there is an art in being a good reader?—to say nothing of expending time to become such. This lamentable situation has naturally an effect upon the author, who, in my opinion, does well to write like Clemens Alexandrinus[89] in such a way that the heretics cannot understand what he writes.

An inquisitive woman reader who looks at the conclusion of every book she finds on her bed-table, in order to see whether the lovers get one another in the end, will here be disappointed; for ordinarily the lovers do get one another, but my friend, though he too is a male, gets no one. Now since it is evident that this is not due to a transient and accidental circumstance, the matter becomes pretty serious for the marriageable girls anxious to be married, who merely by being compelled to strike off the list one single male see the likelihood of fulfilling their expectation somewhat diminished.—An anxious paterfamilias will perhaps be fearful that his son might go the same way as my friend, and will therefore express the opinion that the book does not leave a harmonious impression, forasmuch as it does not furnish a ready-made uniform which will fit any musketeer.—An ephemeral genius will perhaps find that "the exception" creates too many difficulties for himself and takes the thing too seriously.—A genial housewife will seek in vain for a glorification of the trivialities of the sitting-room or of the gossip of the tea-table.—A staunch champion of reality will perhaps be of the opinion that the whole thing turns upon nothing.—An experienced matchmaker will regard the book as a failure, since the real interest would be to find out how a girl ought to be constituted "to make such a man happy"; for that there must be such a girl, or at least must have been, she convinces herself in a way which is thoroughly satisfactory to her.—His Reverence affirms roundly that there is too much philosophy in the book, whereas the thoughful eye of His Right Reverence seeks in vain for the genuine speculative interest which the flock, especially in our days, needs so sorely.—My dear reader, we can just as well say this between ourselves as it were, for thou canst understand that I do not mean to say that all these verdicts might in reality be expressed, seeing that the book will not have many readers.

The ordinary reviewer will find in this book the opportunity he desires to elucidate the fact that it is not a tragedy, a comedy, a romance, an epic, an epigram, or a novel; and will also count it unpardonable that one tries in vain to count 1, 2, 3.[90] He will hardly be able to follow the development of thought, for it is an inverted development. The tendency of the book will certainly not commend itself to him either, for in general reviewers explain existence in such a way that both the universal and the particular are annulled. Above all, it is expecting too much of an ordinary reviewer to suppose that he might have an interest in the dialectical struggle by which the exception breaks away from the universal, in the prolix and very complicated procedure by which the exception fights his way through and asserts himself as a justified exception—for the unjustified exception is recognizable precisely by the fact that he wants to get around the universal.[91] This strife is exceedingly dialectical, having infinite nuances; it postulates absolute readiness in handling the dialectic of the universal, it requires swiftness in the imitation of movements, in short, it is as difficult as putting a man to death and leaving him alive. On the one side stands the exception, on the other the universal, and the strife itself is a strange conflict between the wrath and impatience of the universal at the hubbub the exception causes, and its amatory predilection for the exception. For fundamentally the universal rejoices just as much over the exception as heaven rejoices over one sinner that repenteth, more than over the ninety and nine just persons. On the other side the insubordination and defiance of the exception is in conflict with its weakness and morbidity. The whole thing is a wrestling match[92] in which the universal breaks with the exception, breaks with it in strife, and strengthens it by this conflict. If the exception is unable to endure the distress, the universal does not help it, any more than heaven helps a sinner who cannot endure the pain of repentance. The earnest and resolute exception (which though in conflict with the universal is nevertheless a scion from its root) maintains itself. The situation is as follows. The exception thinks also the universal when it thinks itself, it labors also for the universal when it elaborates itself, it explains the universal when it explains itself. If one would study the universal thoroughly, one has only to look for the justified exception, which manifests everything more clearly than does the universal itself. The justified exception is reconciled with the universal; the universal is fundamentally polemical against the exception, for it will not evince its predilection before the exception, so to speak, compels it to admit it. If the exception does not possess this power, it is not justified, and therefore it is very shrewd of the universal not to evince its predilection too early. If heaven loves one sinner more than ninety and nine just persons, the sinner doubtless does not know this from the beginning; on the contrary, he is sensible only of heaven's wrath, until at last he, as it were, compels heaven to speak out.

In the course of time one grows weary of the perpetual patter about the universal, always the universal, repeated to the most tedious extreme of insipidity. There are exceptions. If one cannot explain them, neither can one explain the universal. Commonly one does not notice the difficulty because one does not think even the universal with passion but with an easygoing superficiality. On the other hand, the exception thinks the universal with serious passion.

When one thinks of the universal in this way, a new order of rank and precedence emerges, and the exception, poor fellow, in case he is fit for anything, comes again to honors and dignity.

Such an exception is a poet. He represents the transition to the more properly aristocratic exceptions, namely, the religious exceptions. The poet is generally an exception. People commonly rejoice over such a man and over his productions. I think therefore it might be worth while for once to bring such a figure into being.[93] The young man whom I have brought into being is a poet. More than this I am unable to do; for at the utmost I can get as far as to imagine a poet and through my imagination produce him. I cannot become a poet myself, and moreover my interests lie elsewhere. I have had a purely aesthetic and psychological interest in this task. I have brought my own person into the theme; but if thou, my dear reader, wilt look more closely, thou wilt easily see that I am only a serviceable spirit and am far from being indifferent to the young man, as he fears. This was a misunderstanding to which I gave occasion in order by this means to bring him out. Every movement I have made is made only in order to throw light upon him; I have constantly had him *in mente,* every word of mine is either ventriloquism or is uttered with reference to him. Even where jest and frolicsomeness seem to rollick regardlessly, they always have regard to him; even where all ends in melancholy, there is a hint about him, about his condition. For this reason all movements take place lyrically, and what I say about myself one is to understand obscurely of him, or by what I say one is to understand him better. Thus I have done for him what I could—just as now in what I am about to say I try to be of service to thee, dear reader, by being again a different person.

A poet's life begins in conflict with the whole of existence. The gist of it is to find an appeasement or a justification; for in the first conflict he must always be defeated, and if he is bent upon triumphing at once, he is an unjustified exception. Now my poet finds a justification precisely in the fact that existence absolves him at the instant when he would as it were annihilate himself. His soul now gains religious tone. This is what really supports him, although it never gets to the point of breaking through. The dithyrambic joy in his last letter is an example of this, for the joy is indubitably grounded in a religious sentiment, which remains however an inward experience. He keeps the religious sentiment as a secret he is unable to explain, although this secret helps him poetically to explain reality. He explains the universal as repetition, and yet he himself understands repetition in a different sense; for while reality becomes repetition, yet for him his own consciousness raised to the second power is repetition. He has had what essentially belongs to a poet, a love experience; but it is entirely ambiguous: happy/unhappy, comic/tragic. With reference to the girl it can all be interpreted comically; for since it was principally sympathy which moved him, his suffering was due in great part to the fact that the loved one suffered. If in this respect he was under a misapprehension, the comic aspect dominates. If he has regard to himself, the tragic aspect becomes prominent, as it does also in another sense when he pictures the loved one ideally. He has retained an ideal conception of the whole love affair, to which he is able to give any expression whatever, but as sentimentally defined, because he possesses no factual evidence. He has therefore a fact of consciousness, or rather he has no fact of consciousness but a dialectical elasticity which will make him productive in the realm of sentiment. While this productivity remains his utmost attainment, he is sustained by something unutterably religious. Thus in the earlier letters, in some of them especially, the movement came much closer to a really religious conclusion; but the instant the temporary suspension is lifted he gets himself again, now however as a poet, and the religious sinks down to the bottom, that is, it remains as an unutterable substratum.

If he had had a deeper religious background, he would not have become a poet. Then everything would have acquired for him religious significance. The event in which he was ensnared would still have had significance for him, but then the shock would have come from higher spheres, and then also he would have been in possession of a very different sort of authority, even though it were bought by sufferings still more painful; he then would have acted with an iron consistency and firmness such as he did not show, he then would have gained a fact of consciousness to which he could constantly hold and which would never become ambiguous to him but would be profound earnestness because he himself had posited it by virtue of a God-relationship. The same instant the whole question about the temporal would have become indifferent to him; what is called reality would in a deeper sense be of no importance to him. He would have drained off religiously all the dreadful consequences contained in that occurrence. Though reality were to turn out differently, it would not change him essentially; even if the worst were to come to pass, it would not dismay him more than he already was dismayed. He would then have understood with religious fear and trembling, but also with trust and confidence, what he had done from the very first, and what as a consequence of this he was morally bound to do later, even though this obligation were to prompt the strangest behavior. On the other hand it is characteristic of the young man as a poet that he never could make thoroughly clear to himself what he had done, precisely because in the outward and visible aspect he wants to see it and does not want to see it, or in the outward and visible aspect he does not want to see it, and therefore wants to see it and does not want to see it. A religious individual, on the contrary, reposes in himself and disdains all the childish pranks of reality.

My dear reader, thou wilt understand that the young man is the focus of interest, whereas I am a transitory figure, like a midwife in relation to the child she has brought to birth. And such in fact is my position, for I have as it were brought him to birth, and therefore as the older person I do the talking. My personality is a presupposition psychologically necessary to force him out, while my personality will never be able to get to the point he has reached, for the primitive power by which he advances is a new and different factor. Therefore from the beginning he has been in good hands, although I have often had to tease him in order that he might make himself visible. At the first glance I saw that he was a poet—for this reason, if for no other, that an occurrence which, if it had happened to a commonplace man would quietly have come to nothing, assumed in his case the proportions of a cosmic event.

Although I often do the talking, thou, my dear reader, wilt everywhere recognize that thou art reading about him; for thou hast understanding of the heartfelt emotions and conditions of the soul, and it is for this reason I call thee "dear." So thou wilt understand why the transitions are so various, and even though thou art taken aback when now and then a douche of sentiments suddenly descends upon thee, thou wilt afterwards see how everything is variously modified to fit together, and wilt see also that the particular moods are fairly correct, which is a capital consideration where the lyrical element is so important. Thou wilt perhaps from time to time be disturbed by an apparently idle witticism or by an indolent expression of defiance, but afterwards perhaps thou wilt be reconciled to this.

Devotedly thine,

CONSTANTINE CONSTANTIUS.

EDITOR'S NOTES

For these notes I am chiefly indebted, as usual, to the editors of the latest Danish edition of Kierkegaard's works. I do not place them at the foot of the page, because I would not mar the appearance of the page. Kierkegaard himself used very few footnotes in the works which he regarded as "aesthetic" or literary. In this case there is only one.

1 Referring to his doctrine of the "monad," to which he ascribed an obscure intuition ("perception") of the whole subsequent development, so that it could be said that "the present is pregnant with the future." Cf. *Theodicy* §360.

2 The author is S.K. himself, for he quotes the conclusion of one of the "Diapsalmata" in *Either/Or*. (Anchor Edition, Vol I, pp. 39f.)

3 Act iii. Scene 12 of a drama of that name, in which the celebrated Neapolitan soprano Farinelli (1705-1838) rouses Louis XV from his apathy to music and draws Philip V of Spain out of his somber melancholy.

4 The manuscript read: "which I am not abusing, for he is dead."

5 In the Preface to the *Fables*.

6 In *Either/Or* S.K. sketched a full-length portrait of Elvira, one of the victims of Don Juan (Anchor Edition, Vol. I, pp. 188-202).

7 Restitution to the original condition.

8 The manuscript reads: "he shot himself."

9 It means overflowed—the phrase is from Goethe's *Faust*, I. 2409.

10 The manuscript read: "death"—instead of "disappearance."

11 Referring more especially to Plato's *Parmenides*. Cf. the Interlude in the *Fragments*.

12 Motion or change. Cf. Plato's *Parmenides* and Aristotle's *Physics* III. 1.

13 Georg Hamann was the German author whom S.K. admired above all. This passage (which here is quoted in German) is to be found in his *Werke* (Roth's ed.) I p. 467. The Greek phrases mean: "in a human way," and "in an absolute way."

14 S.K.'s favorite professor, Poul Møller, entitled a book of his *Straw Thoughts*.

15 A prominent member of the society of political liberals which celebrated annually the establishment on May 28, 1831, of the new constitution of the Danish Parliament. He incurred S.K.'s displeasure for his liberal views, especially for his speech before this society on May 28, 1837, just after S.K. had won some fame by several newspaper articles of a conservative tendency. In 1840 Ussing withdrew from the liberal opposition, became Professor of Jurisprudence in

the University, and cherished political ambitions.

16 The inhabitants of a small island east of Jutland were proverbial in Copenhagen for their naïve simplicity. They were ridiculed in a publication of 1827: "Report of the Wise Deeds and Bold Exploits of the Inhabitants of Mol." S.K.'s account of his suffering is not altogether fanciful, for he wrote to his friend Boesen soon after arriving in Berlin on his second visit, "The day after my arrival I was very bad, my knees ready to sink under me."

17 S.K. did in fact return to his old lodgings, and he found that his bachelor landlord had in the meantime taken a wife. Cf. my *Kierkegaard*, pp. 253*ff*.

18 Such is the title of Judge William's second letter in the Second Part of *Either/Or*.

19 Remember, O man, that thou art dust and to dust shalt thou return.

20 Railways were new, and the tunnel under the Thames was opened only on May 25, 1843.

21 Over the stage of the Royal Theater in Copenhagen was written in Danish: "Not for pleasure only."

22 Two well known restaurants in Copenhagen, the first of which was frequented by students.

23 A musical comedy in three acts by Nestroy, first given in 1843.

24 The *Posse* was a kind of farce which became popular in Berlin about 1840.

25 Color prints, to which S.K. alludes in *Training in Christianity*. Cf. my *Kierkegaard*, p. 39.

26 Has not been identified.

27 Plato's *Phaedrus*.

28 A favorite Berlin actor (d. 1866).

29 A Danish poet (1803-1866).

30 A Danish actor who in a vaudeville with this title by J. L. Heiberg played the rôle of Solomon Goldkalb.

31 An annual fair in the forest known as *Dyrehavn* near Copenhagen.

32 S.K. says in another place, "People nowadays go to church to be entertained and to the theater to be edified." Cf. *Either/Or*, Vol. I, essay on "The Ancient Tragical Motif as reflected in the Modern."

33 I do not know who it was who "conspired to make eternity more terrible than time," unless it was Emanuel Swedenborg by his description of "Heaven and Hell"; but today in America the notion of eternal peace is banished in favor of "the life of perfect service," although the Gospel promises that those who serve here ("interim ethics") shall reign there.

34 The German poet Ewald inscribed on his coffee urn verses to this effect: "Like friendship, so thy juice should be, thou noble Mocha fruit, pure and strong and warm . . . and not abused."

35 According to the *Aeneid* IV 697, the goddess of the underworld could consign no one to death till she had plucked a hair from the head.

36 Socrates always said "the same thing in the same way."

37 A German poet (1786-1862). The Danish editors remark that this passage has not been identified. No wonder, for I remember reading it in an Islandic saga, a tragic story of a feud, in consequence of which the hero had to leave his home to save his life, but because of the accident here described returned to it and was killed. S.K.

refers to it in his *Journal* (II A 233) and associates it with his conversion.

38 In J. L. Heiberg *Kjøge Huskors*, Scene 46.

39 In my *Kierkegaard*, pp. 174*f*., where the following passage is translated, I express the opinion that here S.K. is parodying his own experience of conversion, the "indescribable joy" of May 19, 1838.

40 *Troilus and Cressida*, Act i. Scene 2. By the time Tieck has labored to translate this passage into German, and from this S.K. has turned it into Danish, and I back into English, it hardly can be denied that by our combined labor we have improved upon the English bard. For Shakespeare wrote:

> "He has not past three or four hairs on his chin.
> A tapster's arithmetic may soon bring
> His particulars therein to a total."

41 A persuader to die—a name given to the Cyrenian philosopher Hegesias (fourth century B.C.), who denied the possibility of enjoyment in life and talked so alluringly of death that several of his adherents committed suicide.

42 Note that from this point on repetition is regarded as a religious experience. Cf. the Introduction.

43 Cf. Horace, *Epist.* I.ii.9.

44 Expectation of what one might be able to do.

45 His defense was that he would not be able to preserve silence if he were initiated into the mysteries; for if they were bad, he must dissuade others, and if they were good he must encourage them to join.

46 To understand this passage one must remember Regina's behavior when S.K. sent back the ring: she affirmed that she would die.

47 Has immediate reference to Heiberg's play, "The Soul after Death—An Apocalyptic Comedy," which Professor Martensen in his review of it described as "Aristophanic," alluding to *The Frogs*, which depicted satirically the state of the soul after death, as did Lucian also in his *Dialogues of the Dead*.

48 The term was applied to members of the mendicant orders who acquired the degree of doctor on easy terms; but S.K. is thinking here of a more modern instance, the German *doctores bollati* who received their degrees from the Counts Palatinate without a university examination.

49 There is an intentional confusion here between real death and the feigned dying of a lover, a theme which Constantine Constantius develops in his speech at "The Banquet" in the *Stages on Life's Way*, pp. 66*ff*.

50 A play on words which cannot be rendered. *Ophævelse* means a fuss, a hubbub—used here because *ophæve* (*aufheben*) was Hegel's term for the accomplishment of the transition from the "position" to its negation by means of mediation.

51 A reader who is acquainted with S.K.'s story will recognize that he actually did what the young man professes he lacks courage to do. He was a strange combination of the cold and calculating Constantine, and the timid and sensitive young man.

52 A reference to Regina's behavior when S.K. sent back the ring with a brief note. Instead of accepting the situation, she hastened alone to

his apartment (thereby, as he thought, compromising herself) and left a note adjuring him by all that is holy etc.

53 *Adressavisen,* No. 85, for April 10, 1843.

54 So called for the uniform furnished by an orphan asylum.

55 From a poem, "The Pyre of Love," by Shack Stoffelt.

56 The author has not been identified. The meaning is:

The clouds are driving back and forth,
They are so tired with such a weight;
Then roaringly they plunge them down,
The bosom of the earth's their tomb.

57 In the manuscript the name was given here as Alphonse—evidently before S.K. had made up his mind to leave the young man nameless.

58 Job 1:21. Words which were memorable to S.K. because he heard his father utter them in all sincerity when in quick succession death had taken away three of his children. He took it as the text for one of the *Four Edifying Discourses* published on December 6, 1843, about two months after the publication of *Repetition.*

59 Job 29:4*ff*.

60 Job 7:11.

61 Job 9:3.

62 Job 1 and 2.

63 Job 1:2.

64 S.K. coins a hybrid word, *"Seelenverkooper"* (Dutch *Zielverkooper,* German *Seelenverkaufer*) to describe the touts or lodging-house keepers who kidnap drunken sailors and sell them to a ship.

65 *Pro Roscio* 30, 84: "who profits–"

66 One who knows S.K.'s works will recognize here the theme of two-thirds of the *Stages,* entitled "Guilty?"/"Not Guilty?". I wish he had been able to content himself with this briefer exposition of it.

67 Cap. 6, iii §2B and Cap. 1 §2. *Balles Lærebog* was a manual of Christian doctrine and morality which S.K. must have learnt by rote in his childhood, for he frequently quotes it jestingly.

68 Character in Holberg's *Erasmus Montanus,* a well known comedy.

69 *Gudshaandsplaster*—the name of what presumably was then regarded in Denmark as a sovereign remedy.

70 On the voyage to Troy the Greeks left him behind on the island of Lemnos because he was suffering from an incurable snake-bite, and they could not bear to hear his shrieks.

71 Job 2:13.

72 Job 16:21—translated from the Danish version.

73 Job 19:21.

74 Job 13:4.

75 Job 6:5.

76 Job 29:4.

77 Job 42:10,11.

78 It is to be remembered that *Either/Or* concludes with a sermon on "The edification in the thought that before God we are always in the wrong."

79 Job 8.

80 In fact S.K. did ask it, but Regina would not give it. She is to be taught by this what magnanimity is.

81 Criminals who according to the old law were sentenced to death were "by the King's grace" remanded to the penitentiary for terms of various lengths.

82 The Danes talked of "laughing in one's beard"—instead of "up one's sleeve" as we do.

83 Here ten pages were torn from the manuscript, and what follows was written to replace the original ending—after S.K. learned of Regina's engagement to another.

84 The allusion is to a story recorded in the *Journal* (II A 378): "As he rode up to him he whispered, 'Major, you should turn about'; whereupon the major shouted in a loud voice of command, 'Whole battalion, right-about face,' and therewith he found himself in just as wrong a position, not to speak of the fact that the whole battalion got into the wrong position. That is the misfortune with the politicians; they are always crying 'Whole battalion!' whereas it is only they that ought to do the about-face."

85 Alas, this describes exactly what Regina did. It is only too plain that these four pages were written in the mood of exasperation prompted by the first news of Regina's engagement—and there were more scornful passages in the manuscript, which he had the grace to erase before it was sent to the printer.

86 Job 1:2 and 42:13.

87 A goddess of childbirth. An entry in the *Journal* (the reference to which I have lost) makes it clear that S.K. was thinking of Regina's folded hands.

88 In the manuscript the date given is "July 1843."

89 In his *Stromateis* he often says that he presents the Christian doctrine in a disguised form so that it might not be misunderstood and abused by the uninitiated, but he does not speak expressly of heretics.

90 We are to understand Hegel's three stages: position, negation, mediation.

91 The problem of the exception and the universal is thrashed out in the Second Part of *Either/Or*. No dialectician could delve so deep into this problem unless it was to him an excruciating personal problem, as it was to S.K.

92 *Brydning* means wrestling match, but literally it is "breaking," and so there is a play on words.

93 In the same way Frater Taciturnus in the *Stages* would make one believe at the end that the young man, Quidam, whom he had depicted so realistically, and also the diary which he fished out of the lake, were figments of his imagination. Of course such mystification is characteristic of S.K.'s "intriguing pate," but in this instance it is clear enough that he was intent upon establishing an alibi, that is to say, he desired to distract attention from the only too obvious autobiographical character of this work by representing that this very real young man had no historical existence but was merely his invention, or rather that he was even more remote from reality, being the invention of the character whom he invented, Constantine Constantius.

INDEX

Revised March, 1964

harper torchbooks

HUMANITIES AND SOCIAL SCIENCES

American Studies

JOHN R. ALDEN: The American Revolution, 1775-1783.† *Illus.* TB/3011

RAY STANNARD BAKER: Following the Color Line: *An Account of Negro Citizenship in the American Democracy.‡ Illus. Introduction by Dewey Grantham, Jr.* TB/3053

RAY A. BILLINGTON: The Far Western Frontier, 1830-1860.† *Illus.* TB/3012

JOSEPH L. BLAU, Ed.: Cornerstones of Religious Freedom in America. *Selected Basic Documents, Court Decisions and Public Statements. Enlarged and revised edition with new Intro. by Editor* TB/118

RANDOLPH S. BOURNE: War and the Intellectuals: *Collected Essays, 1915-1919.‡ Edited with an Introduction by Carl Resek* TB/3043

A. RUSSELL BUCHANAN: The United States and World War II. † *Illus.* Volume I TB/3044; Volume II TB/3045

ABRAHAM CAHAN: The Rise of David Levinsky: *a novel. Introduction by John Higham* TB/1028

JOSEPH CHARLES: The Origins of the American Party System TB/1049

T. C. COCHRAN & WILLIAM MILLER: The Age of Enterprise: *A Social History of Industrial America* TB/1054

FOSTER RHEA DULLES: America's Rise to World Power, 1898-1954.† *Illus.* TB/3021

W. A. DUNNING: Reconstruction, Political and Economic, 1865-1877 TB/1073

CLEMENT EATON: The Growth of Southern Civilization, 1790-1860.† *Illus.* TB/3040

HAROLD U. FAULKNER: Politics, Reform and Expansion, 1890-1900.† *Illus.* TB/3020

LOUIS FILLER: The Crusade against Slavery, 1830-1860.† *Illus.* TB/3029

EDITORS OF FORTUNE: America in the Sixties: *the Economy and the Society. Two-color charts* TB/1015

LAWRENCE HENRY GIPSON: The Coming of the Revolution, 1763-1775.† *Illus.* TB/3007

FRANCIS J. GRUND: Aristocracy in America: *Jacksonian Democracy* TB/1001

OSCAR HANDLIN, Editor: This Was America: *As Recorded by European Travelers to the Western Shore in the Eighteenth, Nineteenth, and Twentieth Cenuries. Illus.* TB/1119

MARCUS LEE HANSEN: The Atlantic Migration: 1607-1860. *Edited by Arthur M. Schlesinger; Introduction by Oscar Handlin* TB/1052

MARCUS LEE HANSEN: The Immigrant in American History. *Edited with a Foreword by Arthur Schlesinger, Sr.* TB/1120

JOHN D. HICKS: Republican Ascendancy, 1921-1933.† *Illus.* TB/3041

JOHN HIGHAM, Ed.: The Reconstruction of American History TB/1068

ROBERT H. JACKSON: The Supreme Court in the American System of Government TB/1106

THOMAS JEFFERSON: Notes on the State of Virginia.‡ *Introduction by Thomas Perkins Abernethy* TB/3052

WILLIAM E. LEUCHTENBURG: Franklin D. Roosevelt and the New Deal, 1932-1940.† *Illus.* TB/3025

LEONARD W. LEVY: Freedom of Speech and Press in Early American History: *Legacy of Suppression* TB/1109

ARTHUR S. LINK: Woodrow Wilson and the Progressive Era, 1910-1917.† *Illus.* TB/3023

BERNARD MAYO: Myths and Men: *Patrick Henry, George Washington, Thomas Jefferson* TB/1108

JOHN C. MILLER: The Federalist Era, 1789-1801.† *Illus.* TB/3027

PERRY MILLER & T. H. JOHNSON, Editors: The Puritans: *A Sourcebook of Their Writings* Volume I TB/1093; Volume II TB/1094

GEORGE E. MOWRY: The Era of Theodore Roosevelt and the Birth of Modern America, 1900-1912.† *Illus.* TB/3022

WALLACE NOTESTEIN: The English People on the Eve of Colonization, 1603-1630.† *Illus.* TB/3006

RUSSEL BLAINE NYE: The Cultural Life of the New Nation, 1776-1801.† *Illus.* TB/3026

GEORGE E. PROBST, Ed.: The Happy Republic: *A Reader in Tocqueville's America* TB/1060

FRANK THISTLETHWAITE: America and the Atlantic Community: *Anglo-American Aspects, 1790-1850* TB/1107

† The New American Nation Series, edited by Henry Steele Commager and Richard B. Morris.

‡ American Perspectives series, edited by Bernard Wishy and William E. Leuchtenburg.

* The Rise of Modern Europe series, edited by William L. Langer.

** Researches in the Social, Cultural, and Behavioral Sciences, edited by Benjamin Nelson

§ The Library of Religion and Culture, edited by Benjamin Nelson.

Σ Harper Modern Science Series, edited by James R. Newman.

° Not for sale in Canada.

TWELVE SOUTHERNERS: I'll Take My Stand: *The South and the Agrarian Tradition. Introduction by Louis D. Rubin, Jr.; Biographical Essays by Virginia Rock* TB/1072

A. F. TYLER: Freedom's Ferment: *Phases of American Social History from the Revolution to the Outbreak of the Civil War. Illus.* TB/1074

GLYNDON G. VAN DEUSEN: The Jacksonian Era, 1828-1848.† *Illus.* TB/3028

WALTER E. WEYL: The New Democracy: *An Essay on Certain Political and Economic Tendencies in the United States.‡ Introduction by Charles Forcey* TB/3042

LOUIS B. WRIGHT: The Cultural Life of the American Colonies, 1607-1763.† *Illus.* TB/3005

LOUIS B. WRIGHT: Culture on the Moving Frontier TB/1053

Anthropology & Sociology

BERNARD BERELSON, Ed.: The Behavioral Sciences Today TB/1127

JOSEPH B. CASAGRANDE, Ed.: In the Company of Man: *20 Portraits of Anthropological Informants. Illus.* TB/3047

W. E. LE GROS CLARK: The Antecedents of Man: *An Introduction to the Evolution of the Primates.° Illus.* TB/559

ALLISON DAVIS & JOHN DOLLARD: Children of Bondage: *The Personality Development of Negro Youth in the Urban South*** TB/3049

ST. CLAIR DRAKE & HORACE R. CAYTON: Black Metropolis: *A Study of Negro Life in a Northern City. Introduction by Everett C. Hughes. Tables, maps, charts and graphs* Volume I TB/1086; Volume II TB/1087

CORA DU BOIS: The People of Alor. *New Preface by the author. Illus.* Volume I TB/1042; Volume II TB/1043

LEON FESTINGER, HENRY W. RIECKEN & STANLEY SCHACHTER: When Prophecy Fails: *A Social and Psychological Account of a Modern Group that Predicted the Destruction of the World*** TB/1132

RAYMOND FIRTH, Ed.: Man and Culture: *An Evaluation of the Work of Bronislaw Malinowski*** ° TB/1133

L. S. B. LEAKEY: Adam's Ancestors: *The Evolution of Man and his Culture. Illus.* TB/1019

KURT LEWIN: Field Theory in Social Science: *Selected Theoretical Papers.** Edited with a Foreword by Dorwin Cartwright* TB/1135

ROBERT H. LOWIE: Primitive Society. *Introduction by Fred Eggan* TB/1056

BENJAMIN NELSON: Religious Traditions and the Spirit of Capitalism: *From the Church Fathers to Jeremy Bentham* TB/1130

TALCOTT PARSONS & EDWARD A. SHILS, Editors: Toward a General Theory of Action: *Theoretical Foundations for the Social Sciences* TB/1083

JOHN H. ROHRER & MUNRO S. EDMONSON, Eds.: The Eighth Generation Grows Up: *Cultures and Personalities of New Orleans Negroes*** TB/3050

ARNOLD ROSE: The Negro in America: *The Condensed Version of Gunnar Myrdal's* An American Dilemma. *New Introduction by the Author; Foreword by Gunnar Myrdal* TB/3048

KURT SAMUELSSON: Religion and Economic Action: *A Critique of Max Weber.** °* *Trans. by E. G. French; Ed. with Intro. by D. C. Coleman* TB/1131

PITIRIM SOROKIN: Contemporary Sociological Theories. *Through The First Quarter of the 20th Century* TB/3046

MAURICE R. STEIN: The Eclipse of Community: *An Interpretation of American Studies. New Introduction by the Author* TB/1128

SIR EDWARD TYLOR: The Origins of Culture. *Part I of "Primitive Culture."§ Introduction by Paul Radin* TB/33

SIR EDWARD TYLOR: Religion in Primitive Culture. *Part II of "Primitive Culture."§ Introduction by Paul Radin* TB/34

W. LLOYD WARNER & Associates: Democracy in Jonesville: *A Study in Quality and Inequality*** TB/1129

W. LLOYD WARNER: Social Class in America: *The Evaluation of Status* TB/1013

Art and Art History

EMILE MÂLE: The Gothic Image: *Religious Art in France of the Thirteenth Century.§ 190 illus.* TB/44

ERWIN PANOFSKY: Studies in Iconology: *Humanistic Themes in the Art of the Renaissance. 180 illustrations* TB/1077

ALEXANDRE PIANKOFF: The Shrines of Tut-Ankh-Amon. *Edited by N. Rambova. 117 illus.* TB/2011

JEAN SEZNEC: The Survival of the Pagan Gods: *The Mythological Tradition and Its Place in Renaissance Humanism and Art. 108 illustrations* TB/2004

OTTO VON SIMSON: The Gothic Cathedral: *Origins of Gothic Architecture and the Medieval Concept of Order. 58 illus.* TB/2018

HEINRICH ZIMMER: Myths and Symbols in Indian Art and Civilization. *70 illustrations* TB/2005

Business, Economics & Economic History

REINHARD BENDIX: Work and Authority in Industry: *Ideologies of Management in the Course of Industrialization* TB/3035

THOMAS C. COCHRAN: The American Business System: *A Historical Perspective, 1900-1955* TB/1080

ROBERT DAHL & CHARLES E. LINDBLOM: Politics, Economics, and Welfare: *Planning and Politico-Economic Systems Resolved into Basic Social Processes* TB/3037

PETER F. DRUCKER: The New Society: *The Anatomy of Industrial Order* TB/1082

ROBERT L. HEILBRONER: The Great Ascent: *The Struggle for Economic Development in Our Time* TB/3030

ABBA P. LERNER: Everybody's Business: *A Re-examination of Current Assumptions in Economics and Public Policy* TB/3051

PAUL MANTOUX: The Industrial Revolution in the Eighteenth Century: *The Beginnings of the Modern Factory System in England°* TB/1079

WILLIAM MILLER, Ed.: Men in Business: *Essays on the Historical Role of the Entrepreneur* TB/1081

PERRIN STRYKER: The Character of the Executive: *Eleven Studies in Managerial Qualities* TB/1041

PIERRE URI: Partnership for Progress: *A Program for Transatlantic Action* TB/3036

Contemporary Culture

JACQUES BARZUN: The House of Intellect TB/1051

JOHN U. NEF: Cultural Foundations of Industrial Civilization TB/1024

PAUL VALÉRY: The Outlook for Intelligence TB/2016

History: General

L. CARRINGTON GOODRICH: A Short History of the Chinese People. *Illus.* TB/3015

BERNARD LEWIS: The Arabs in History TB/1029

SIR PERCY SYKES: A History of Exploration.° *Introduction by John K. Wright* TB/1046

History: Ancient and Medieval

A. ANDREWES: The Greek Tyrants TB/1103

HELEN CAM: England before Elizabeth TB/1026

NORMAN COHN: The Pursuit of the Millennium: *Revolutionary Messianism in medieval and Reformation Europe and its bearing on modern Leftist and Rightist totalitarian movements* TB/1037

G. G. COULTON: Medieval Village, Manor, and Monastery TB/1022

F. L. GANSHOF: Feudalism TB/1058

J. M. HUSSEY: The Byzantine World TB/1057

SAMUEL NOAH KRAMER: Sumerian Mythology TB/1055

FERDINAND LOT: The End of the Ancient World and the Beginnings of the Middle Ages. *Introduction by Glanville Downey* TB/1044

HENRY OSBORN TAYLOR: The Classical Heritage of the Middle Ages. *Foreword and Biblio. by Kenneth M. Setton* [Formerly listed as TB/48 under the title *The Emergence of Christian Culture in the West*] TB/1117

J. M. WALLACE-HADRILL: The Barbarian West: *The Early Middle Ages, A.D. 400-1000* TB/1061

History: Renaissance & Reformation

R. R. BOLGAR: The Classical Heritage and Its Beneficiaries: *From the Carolingian Age to the End of the Renaissance* TB/1125

JACOB BURCKHARDT: The Civilization of the Renaissance in Italy. *Introduction by Benjamin Nelson and Charles Trinkaus. Illus.* Volume I TB/40 Volume II TB/41

ERNST CASSIRER: The Individual and the Cosmos in Renaissance Philosophy. *Translated with an Introduction by Mario Domandi* TB/1097

EDWARD P. CHEYNEY: The Dawn of a New Era, 1250-1453.* *Illus.* TB/3002

WALLACE K. FERGUSON, et al.: Facets of the Renaissance TB/1098

WALLACE K. FERGUSON, et al.: The Renaissance: *Six Essays. Illus.* TB/1084

MYRON P. GILMORE: The World of Humanism, 1453-1517.* *Illus.* TB/3003

JOHAN HUIZINGA: Erasmus and the Age of Reformation. *Illus.* TB/19

ULRICH VON HUTTEN, et al.: On the Eve of the Reformation: *"Letters of Obscure Men." Introduction by Hajo Holborn* TB/1124

PAUL O. KRISTELLER: Renaissance Thought: *The Classic, Scholastic, and Humanist Strains* TB/1048

NICCOLÒ MACHIAVELLI: History of Florence and of the Affairs of Italy: *from the earliest times to the death of Lorenzo the Magnificent. Introduction by Felix Gilbert* TB/1027

ALFRED VON MARTIN: Sociology of the Renaissance. *Introduction by Wallace K. Ferguson* TB/1099

J. E. NEALE: The Age of Catherine de Medici° TB/1085

ERWIN PANOFSKY: Studies in Iconology: *Humanistic Themes in the Art of the Renaissance. 180 illustrations* TB/1077

J. H. PARRY: The Establishment of the European Hegemony: 1415-1715: *Trade and Exploration in the Age of the Renaissance* TB/1045

HENRI PIRENNE: Early Democracies in the Low Countries: *Urban Society and Political Conflict in the Middle Ages and the Renaissance. Introduction by John Mundy* TB/1110

FERDINAND SCHEVILL: The Medici. *Illus.* TB/1010

FERDINAND SCHEVILL: Medieval and Renaissance Florence. *Illus.* Volume I: *Medieval Florence* TB/1090 Volume II: *The Coming of Humanism and the Age of the Medici* TB/1091

G. M. TREVELYAN: England in the Age of Wycliffe, 1368-1520° TB/1112

VESPASIANO: Renaissance Princes, Popes, and Prelates: *The Vespasiano Memoirs: Lives of Illustrious Men of the XVth Century. Introduction by Myron P. Gilmore* TB/1111

History: Modern European

FREDERICK B. ARTZ: Reaction and Revolution, 1815-1832.* *Illus.* TB/3034

MAX BELOFF: The Age of Absolutism, 1660-1815 TB/1062

ROBERT C. BINKLEY: Realism and Nationalism, 1852-1871.* *Illus.* TB/3038

CRANE BRINTON: A Decade of Revolution, 1789-1799.* *Illus.* TB/3018

J. BRONOWSKI & BRUCE MAZLISH: The Western Intellectual Tradition: *From Leonardo to Hegel* TB/3001

GEOFFREY BRUUN: Europe and the French Imperium, 1799-1814.* *Illus.* TB/3033

ALAN BULLOCK: Hitler, A Study in Tyranny.° *Illus.* TB/1123

E. H. CARR: The Twenty Years' Crisis, 1919-1939: *An Introduction to the Study of International Relations°* TB/1122

WALTER L. DORN: Competition for Empire, 1740-1763.* *Illus.* TB/3032

CARL J. FRIEDRICH: The Age of the Baroque, 1610-1660.* *Illus.* TB/3004

LEO GERSHOY: From Despotism to Revolution, 1763-1789.* *Illus.* TB/3017

ALBERT GOODWIN: The French Revolution TB/1064

CARLTON J. H. HAYES: A Generation of Materialism, 1871-1900.* *Illus.* TB/3039

J. H. HEXTER: Reappraisals in History: *New Views on History and Society in Early Modern Europe* TB/1100

A. R. HUMPHREYS: The Augustan World: *Society, Thought, and Letters in Eighteenth Century England* TB/1105

HANS KOHN, Ed.: The Mind of Modern Russia: *Historical and Political Thought of Russia's Great Age* TB/1065

SIR LEWIS NAMIER: Vanished Supremacies: *Essays on European History, 1812-1918°* TB/1088

JOHN U. NEF: Western Civilization Since the Renaissance: *Peace, War, Industry, and the Arts* TB/1113

FREDERICK L. NUSSBAUM: The Triumph of Science and Reason, 1660-1685.* *Illus.* TB/3009

RAYMOND W. POSTGATE, Ed.: Revolution from 1789 to 1906: *Selected Documents* TB/1063

PENFIELD ROBERTS: The Quest for Security, 1715-1740.* *Illus.* TB/3016

PRISCILLA ROBERTSON: Revolutions of 1848: *A Social History* TB/1025

ALBERT SOREL: Europe Under the Old Regime. *Translated by Francis H. Herrick* TB/1121

N. N. SUKHANOV: The Russian Revolution, 1917: *Eyewitness Account.* Edited by Joel Carmichael
Volume I TB/1066
Volume II TB/1067

JOHN B. WOLF: The Emergence of the Great Powers, 1685-1715.* *Illus.* TB/3010

JOHN B. WOLF: France: 1814-1919: *The Rise of a Liberal-Democratic Society* TB/3019

Intellectual History

HERSCHEL BAKER: The Image of Man: *A Study of the Idea of Human Dignity in Classical Antiquity, the Middle Ages, and the Renaissance* TB/1047

J. BRONOWSKI & BRUCE MAZLISH: The Western Intellectual Tradition: *From Leonardo to Hegel* TB/3001

ERNST CASSIRER: The Individual and the Cosmos in Renaissance Philosophy. *Translated with an Introduction by Mario Domandi* TB/1097

NORMAN COHN: The Pursuit of the Millennium: *Revolutionary Messianism in medieval and Reformation Europe and its bearing on modern Leftist and Rightist totalitarian movements* TB/1037

ARTHUR O. LOVEJOY: The Great Chain of Being: *A Study of the History of an Idea* TB/1009

ROBERT PAYNE: Hubris: *A Study of Pride. Foreword by Sir Herbert Read* TB/1031

BRUNO SNELL: The Discovery of the Mind: *The Greek Origins of European Thought* TB/1018

ERNEST LEE TUVESON: Millennium and Utopia: *A Study in the Background of the Idea of Progress.*** *New Preface by Author* TB/1134

Literature, Poetry, The Novel & Criticism

JAMES BAIRD: Ishmael: *The Art of Melville in the Contexts of International Primitivism* TB/1023

JACQUES BARZUN: The House of Intellect TB/1051

W. J. BATE: From Classic to Romantic: *Premises of Taste in Eighteenth Century England* TB/1036

RACHEL BESPALOFF: On the Iliad TB/2006

R. P. BLACKMUR, et al.: Lectures in Criticism. *Introduction by Huntington Cairns* TB/2003

ABRAHAM CAHAN: The Rise of David Levinsky: *a novel. Introduction by John Higham* TB/1028

ERNST R. CURTIUS: European Literature and the Latin Middle Ages TB/2015

GEORGE ELIOT: Daniel Deronda: *a novel. Introduction by F. R. Leavis* TB/1039

ETIENNE GILSON: Dante and Philosophy TB/1089

ALFRED HARBAGE: As They Liked It: *A Study of Shakespeare's Moral Artistry* TB/1035

STANLEY R. HOPPER, Ed.: Spiritual Problems in Contemporary Literature§ TB/21

A. R. HUMPHREYS: The Augustan World: *Society, Thought, and Letters in Eighteenth Century England*° TB/1105

ALDOUS HUXLEY: Antic Hay & The Gioconda Smile.° *Introduction by Martin Green* TB/3503

ALDOUS HUXLEY: Brave New World & Brave New World Revisited.° *Introduction by C. P. Snow* TB/3501

ALDOUS HUXLEY: Point Counter Point.° *Introduction by C. P. Snow* TB/3502

HENRY JAMES: The Princess Casamassima: *a novel. Introduction by Clinton F. Oliver* TB/1005

HENRY JAMES: Roderick Hudson: *a novel. Introduction by Leon Edel* TB/1016

HENRY JAMES: The Tragic Muse: *a novel. Introduction by Leon Edel* TB/1017

ARNOLD KETTLE: An Introduction to the English Novel. Volume I: *Defoe to George Eliot* TB/1011
Volume II: *Henry James to the Present* TB/1012

JOHN STUART MILL: On Bentham and Coleridge. *Introduction by F. R. Leavis* TB/1070

PERRY MILLER & T. H. JOHNSON, Editors: The Puritans: *A Sourcebook of Their Writings*
Volume I TB/1093
Volume II TB/1094

KENNETH B. MURDOCK: Literature and Theology in Colonial New England TB/99

SAMUEL PEPYS: The Diary of Samuel Pepys.° *Edited by O. F. Morshead. Illustrations by Ernest Shepard* TB/1007

ST.-JOHN PERSE: Seamarks TB/2002

O. E. RÖLVAAG: Giants in the Earth. *Introduction by Einar Haugen* TB/3504

GEORGE SANTAYANA: Interpretations of Poetry and Religion§ TB/9

C. P. SNOW: Time of Hope: *a novel* TB/1040

DOROTHY VAN GHENT: The English Novel: *Form and Function* TB/1050

E. B. WHITE: One Man's Meat. *Introduction by Walter Blair* TB/3505

MORTON DAUWEN ZABEL, Editor: Literary Opinion in America
Volume I TB/3013
Volume II TB/3014

Myth, Symbol & Folklore

JOSEPH CAMPBELL, Editor: Pagan and Christian Mysteries. *Illus.* TB/2013

MIRCEA ELIADE: Cosmos and History: *The Myth of the Eternal Return*§ TB/2050

C. G. JUNG & C. KERÉNYI: Essays on a Science of Mythology: *The Myths of the Divine Child and the Divine Maiden* TB/2014

ERWIN PANOFSKY: Studies in Iconology: *Humanistic Themes in the Art of the Renaissance. 180 illustrations* TB/1077

JEAN SEZNEC: The Survival of the Pagan Gods: *The Mythological Tradition and its Place in Renaissance Humanism and Art. 108 illustrations* TB/2004

HEINRICH ZIMMER: Myths and Symbols in Indian Art and Civilization. *70 illustrations* TB/2005

Philosophy

HENRI BERGSON: Time and Free Will: *An Essay on the Immediate Data of Consciousness*° TB/1021

H. J. BLACKHAM: Six Existentialist Thinkers: *Kierkegaard, Nietzsche, Jaspers, Marcel, Heidegger, Sartre*° TB/1002

ERNST CASSIRER: Rousseau, Kant and Goethe. *Introduction by Peter Gay* TB/1092

FREDERICK COPLESTON: Medieval Philosophy° TB/76

F. M. CORNFORD: From Religion to Philosophy: *A Study in the Origins of Western Speculation*§ TB/20

WILFRID DESAN: The Tragic Finale: *An Essay on the Philosophy of Jean-Paul Sartre* TB/1030

PAUL FRIEDLÄNDER: Plato: *An Introduction* TB/2017

ETIENNE GILSON: Dante and Philosophy TB/1089

WILLIAM CHASE GREENE: Moira: *Fate, Good, and Evil in Greek Thought* TB/1104

W. K. C. GUTHRIE: The Greek Philosophers: *From Thales to Aristotle*° TB/1008

F. H. HEINEMANN: Existentialism and the Modern Predicament TB/28

IMMANUEL KANT: The Doctrine of Virtue, *being Part II of The Metaphysic of Morals. Translated with Notes and Introduction by Mary J. Gregor. Foreword by H. J. Paton* TB/110

IMMANUEL KANT: Lectures on Ethics.§ *Introduction by Lewis W. Beck* TB/105

WILLARD VAN ORMAN QUINE: From a Logical Point of View: *Logico-Philosophical Essays* TB/566

BERTRAND RUSSELL et al.: The Philosophy of Bertrand Russell. *Edited by Paul Arthur Schilpp*
Volume I TB/1095
Volume II TB/1096

L. S. STEBBING: A Modern Introduction to Logic TB/538

ALFRED NORTH WHITEHEAD: Process and Reality: *An Essay in Cosmology* TB/1033

WILHELM WINDELBAND: A History of Philosophy I: *Greek, Roman, Medieval* TB/38

WILHELM WINDELBAND: A History of Philosophy II: *Renaissance, Enlightenment, Modern* TB/39

Philosophy of History

NICOLAS BERDYAEV: The Beginning and the End§ TB/14

NICOLAS BERDYAEV: The Destiny of Man TB/61

WILHELM DILTHEY: Pattern and Meaning in History: *Thoughts on History and Society.° Edited with an Introduction by H. P. Rickman* TB/1075

RAYMOND KLIBANSKY & H. J. PATON, Eds.: Philosophy and History: *The Ernst Cassirer Festschrift. Illus.* TB/1115

JOSE ORTEGA Y GASSET: The Modern Theme. *Introduction by Jose Ferrater Mora* TB/1038

KARL R. POPPER: The Poverty of Historicism° TB/1126

W. H. WALSH: Philosophy of History: *An Introduction* TB/1020

Political Science & Government

JEREMY BENTHAM: The Handbook of Political Fallacies: *Introduction by Crane Brinton* TB/1069

KENNETH E. BOULDING: Conflict and Defense: *A General Theory* TB/3024

CRANE BRINTON: English Political Thought in the Nineteenth Century TB/1071

ROBERT DAHL & CHARLES E. LINDBLOM: Politics, Economics, and Welfare: *Planning and Politico-Economic Systems Resolved into Basic Social Processes* TB/3037

JOHN NEVILLE FIGGIS: Political Thought from Gerson to Grotius: 1414-1625: *Seven Studies. Introduction by Garrett Mattingly* TB/1032

F. L. GANSHOF: Feudalism TB/1058

G. P. GOOCH: English Democratic Ideas in the Seventeenth Century TB/1006

ROBERT H. JACKSON: The Supreme Court in the American System of Government TB/1106

DAN N. JACOBS, Ed.: The New Communist Manifesto *and Related Documents* TB/1078

DAN N. JACOBS & HANS BAERWALD, Eds.: Chinese Communism: *Selected Documents* TB/3031

KINGSLEY MARTIN: French Liberal Thought in the Eighteenth Century: *A Study of Political Ideas from Bayle to Condorcet* TB/1114

JOHN STUART MILL: On Bentham and Coleridge. *Introduction by F. R. Leavis* TB/1070

JOHN B. MORRALL: Political Thought in Medieval Times TB/1076

KARL R. POPPER: The Open Society and Its Enemies
Volume I: *The Spell of Plato* TB/1101
Volume II: *The High Tide of Prophecy: Hegel, Marx, and the Aftermath* TB/1102

JOSEPH A. SCHUMPETER: Capitalism, Socialism and Democracy TB/3008

Psychology

ANTON T. BOISEN: The Exploration of the Inner World: *A Study of Mental Disorder and Religious Experience* TB/87

SIGMUND FREUD: On Creativity and the Unconscious: *Papers on the Psychology of Art, Literature, Love, Religion.§ Intro. by Benjamin Nelson* TB/45

C. JUDSON HERRICK: The Evolution of Human Nature TB/545

ALDOUS HUXLEY: The Devils of Loudun: *A Study in the Psychology of Power Politics and Mystical Religion in the France of Cardinal Richelieu*§° TB/60

WILLIAM JAMES: Psychology: *The Briefer Course. Edited with an Intro. by Gordon Allport* TB/1034

C. G. JUNG: Psychological Reflections. *Edited by Jolande Jacobi* TB/2001

C. G. JUNG: Symbols of Transformation: *An Analysis of the Prelude to a Case of Schizophrenia. Illus.*
Volume I TB/2009
Volume II TB/2010

C. G. JUNG & C. KERÉNYI: Essays on a Science of Mythology: *The Myths of the Divine Child and the Divine Maiden* TB/2014

SOREN KIERKEGAARD: Repetition: *An Essay in Experimental Psychology. Translated with Introduction & Notes by Walter Lowrie* TB/117

ERICH NEUMANN: Amor and Psyche: *The Psychic Development of the Feminine* TB/2012

ERICH NEUMANN: The Origins and History of Consciousness
Volume I *Illus.* TB/2007
Volume II TB/2008

RELIGION

Ancient & Classical

J. H. BREASTED: Development of Religion and Thought in Ancient Egypt. *Introduction by John A. Wilson* TB/57

HENRI FRANKFORT: Ancient Egyptian Religion: *An Interpretation* TB/77

WILLIAM CHASE GREENE: Moira: *Fate, Good and Evil in Greek Thought* TB/1104

G. RACHEL LEVY: Religious Conceptions of the Stone Age *and their Influence upon European Thought. Illus. Introduction by Henri Frankfort* TB/106

MARTIN P. NILSSON: Greek Folk Religion. *Foreword by Arthur Darby Nock* TB/78

ALEXANDRE PIANKOFF: The Shrines of Tut-Ankh-Amon. *Edited by N. Rambova. 117 illus.* TB/2011

H. J. ROSE: Religion in Greece and Rome TB/55

Biblical Thought & Literature

W. F. ALBRIGHT: The Biblical Period from Abraham to Ezra TB/102

C. K. BARRETT, Ed.: The New Testament Background: *Selected Documents* TB/86

C. H. DODD: The Authority of the Bible TB/43

M. S. ENSLIN: Christian Beginnings TB/5

M. S. ENSLIN: The Literature of the Christian Movement TB/6

H. E. FOSDICK: A Guide to Understanding the Bible TB/2

H. H. ROWLEY: The Growth of the Old Testament TB/107

D. WINTON THOMAS, Ed.: Documents from Old Testament Times TB/85

Christianity: Origins & Early Development

EDWARD GIBBON: The Triumph of Christendom in the Roman Empire *(Chaps. XV-XX of "Decline and Fall," J. B. Bury edition).§ Illus.* TB/46

MAURICE GOGUEL: Jesus and the Origins of Christianity.° *Introduction by C. Leslie Mitton*
Volume I: *Prolegomena to the Life of Jesus* TB/65
Volume II: *The Life of Jesus* TB/66

EDGAR J. GOODSPEED: A Life of Jesus TB/1

ADOLF HARNACK: The Mission and Expansion of Christianity *in the First Three Centuries. Introduction by Jaroslav Pelikan* TB/92

R. K. HARRISON: The Dead Sea Scrolls: *An Introduction°* TB/84

EDWIN HATCH: The Influence of Greek Ideas on Christianity.§ *Introduction and Bibliography by Frederick C. Grant* TB /18

ARTHUR DARBY NOCK: Early Gentile Christianity and Its Hellenistic Background TB/111

ARTHUR DARBY NOCK: St. Paul° TB/104

JOHANNES WEISS: Earliest Christianity: *A History of the Period A.D. 30-150. Introduction and Bibilography by Frederick C. Grant* Volume I TB/53
Volume II TB/54

Christianity: The Middle Ages and After

G. P. FEDOTOV: The Russian Religious Mind: *Kievan Christianity, the tenth to the thirteenth centuries* TB/70

ÉTIENNE GILSON: Dante and Philosophy TB/1089

WILLIAM HALLER: The Rise of Puritanism TB/22

JOHAN HUIZINGA: Erasmus and the Age of Reformation. *Illus.* TB/19

A. C. McGIFFERT: Protestant Thought Before Kant. *Preface by Jaroslav Pelikan* TB/93

KENNETH B. MURDOCK: Literature and Theology in Colonial New England TB/99

Judaic Thought & Literature

MARTIN BUBER: Eclipse of God: *Studies in the Relation Between Religion and Philosophy* TB/12

MARTIN BUBER: Moses: *The Revelation and the Covenant* TB/27

MARTIN BUBER: Pointing the Way. *Introduction by Maurice S. Friedman* TB/103

MARTIN BUBER: The Prophetic Faith TB/73

MARTIN BUBER: Two Types of Faith: *the interpenetration of Judaism and Christianity°* TB/75

MAURICE S. FRIEDMAN: Martin Buber: *The Life of Dialogue* TB/64

FLAVIUS JOSEPHUS: The Great Roman-Jewish War, *with* The Life of Josephus. *Introduction by William R. Farmer* TB/74

T. J. MEEK: Hebrew Origins TB/69

Oriental Religions: Far Eastern, Near Eastern

TOR ANDRAE: Mohammed: *The Man and His Faith* TB/62

EDWARD CONZE: Buddhism: *Its Essence and Development.° Foreword by Arthur Waley* TB/58

EDWARD CONZE, et al., Editors: Buddhist Texts Through the Ages TB/113

ANANDA COOMARASWAMY: Buddha and the Gospel of Buddhism TB/119

H. G. CREEL: Confucius and the Chinese Way TB/63

FRANKLIN EDGERTON, Trans. & Ed.: The Bhagavad Gita TB/115

SWAMI NIKHILANANDA, Trans. & Ed.: The Upanishads: *A One-Volume Abridgment* TB/114

Philosophy of Religion

RUDOLF BULTMANN: History and Eschatology: *The Presence of Eternity* TB/91

RUDOLF BULTMANN AND FIVE CRITICS: Kerygma and Myth: *A Theological Debate* TB/80

RUDOLF BULTMANN and KARL KUNDSIN: Form Criticism: *Two Essays on New Testament Research. Translated by Frederick C. Grant* TB/96

MIRCEA ELIADE: The Sacred and the Profane TB/81

LUDWIG FEUERBACH: The Essence of Christianity.§ *Introduction by Karl Barth. Foreword by H. Richard Niebuhr* TB/11

ADOLF HARNACK: What is Christianity?§ *Introduction by Rudolf Bultmann* TB/17

FRIEDRICH HEGEL: On Christianity: *Early Theological Writings. Edited by Richard Kroner and T. M. Knox* TB/79

KARL HEIM: Christian Faith and Natural Science TB/16

IMMANUEL KANT: Religion Within the Limits of Reason Alone.§ *Introduction by Theodore M. Greene and John Silber* TB/67

PIERRE TEILHARD DE CHARDIN: The Phenomenon of Man° TB/83

Religion, Culture & Society

JOSEPH L. BLAU, Ed.: Cornerstones of Religious Freedom in America: *Selected Basic Documents, Court Decisions and Public Statements. Enlarged and revised edition, with new Introduction by the Editor* TB/118

C. C. GILLISPIE: Genesis and Geology: *The Decades before Darwin§* TB/51

BENJAMIN NELSON: Religious Traditions and the Spirit of Capitalism: *From the Church Fathers to Jeremy Bentham* TB/1130

H. RICHARD NIEBUHR: Christ and Culture TB/3

H. RICHARD NIEBUHR: The Kingdom of God in America TB/49

KURT SAMUELSSON: Religion and Economic Action: *A Critique of Max Weber.*** ° *Trans. by E. G. French; Ed. with Intro. by D. C. Coleman* TB/1131

ERNST TROELTSCH: The Social Teaching of the Christian Churches.° *Introduction by H. Richard Niebuhr* Volume I TB/71; Volume II TB/72

Religious Thinkers & Traditions

AUGUSTINE: An Augustine Synthesis. *Edited by Erich Przywara* TB/35

KARL BARTH: Church Dogmatics: *A Selection. Introduction by H. Gollwitzer; Edited by G. W. Bromiley* TB/95

KARL BARTH: Dogmatics in Outline TB/56

KARL BARTH: The Word of God and the Word of Man TB/13

THOMAS CORBISHLEY, S. J.: Roman Catholicism TB/112

ADOLF DEISSMANN: Paul: *A Study in Social and Religious History* TB/15

JOHANNES ECKHART: Meister Eckhart: *A Modern Translation by R. B. Blakney* TB/8

WINTHROP HUDSON: The Great Tradition of the American Churches TB/98

SOREN KIERKEGAARD: Edifying Discourses. *Edited with an Introduction by Paul Holmer* TB/32

SOREN KIERKEGAARD: The Journals of Kierkegaard.° *Edited with an Introduction by Alexander Dru* TB/52

SOREN KIERKEGAARD: The Point of View for My Work as an Author: *A Report to History.*§ *Preface by Benjamin Nelson* TB/88

SOREN KIERKEGAARD: The Present Age.§ *Translated and edited by Alexander Dru. Introduction by Walter Kaufmann* TB/94

SOREN KIERKEGAARD: Purity of Heart. *Translated by Douglas Steere* TB/4

SOREN KIERKEGAARD: Repetition: *An Essay in Experimental Psychology. Translated with Introduction & Notes by Walter Lowrie* TB/117

WALTER LOWRIE: Kierkegaard: *A Life* Volume I TB/89; Volume II TB/90

GABRIEL MARCEL: Homo Viator: *Introduction to a Metaphysic of Hope* TB/97

PERRY MILLER & T. H. JOHNSON, Editors: The Puritans: *A Sourcebook of Their Writings* Volume I TB/1093; Volume II TB/1094

PAUL PFUETZE: Self, Society, Existence: *Human Nature and Dialogue in the Thought of George Herbert Mead and Martin Buber* TB/1059

F. SCHLEIERMACHER: The Christian Faith. *Introduction by Richard R. Niebuhr* Volume I TB/108; Volume II TB/109

F. SCHLEIERMACHER: On Religion: *Speeches to Its Cultured Despisers. Intro. by Rudolf Otto* TB/36

PAUL TILLICH: Dynamics of Faith TB/42

EVELYN UNDERHILL: Worship TB/10

G. VAN DER LEEUW: Religion in Essence and Manifestation: *A Study in Phenomenology. Appendices by Hans H. Penner* Volume I TB/100; Volume II TB/101

NATURAL SCIENCES AND MATHEMATICS

Biological Sciences

CHARLOTTE AUERBACH: The Science of Genetics Σ TB/568

A. BELLAIRS: Reptiles: *Life History, Evolution, and Structure. Illus.* TB/520

LUDWIG VON BERTALANFFY: Modern Theories of Development: *An Introduction to Theoretical Biology* TB/554

LUDWIG VON BERTALANFFY: Problems of Life: *An Evaluation of Modern Biological and Scientific Thought* TB/521

JOHN TYLER BONNER: The Ideas of Biology. Σ *Illus.* TB/570

HAROLD F. BLUM: Time's Arrow and Evolution TB/555

A. J. CAIN: Animal Species and their Evolution. *Illus.* TB/519

WALTER B. CANNON: Bodily Changes in Pain, Hunger, Fear and Rage. *Illus.* TB/562

W. E. LE GROS CLARK: The Antecedents of Man: *An Introduction to the Evolution of the Primates.*° *Illus.* TB/559

W. H. DOWDESWELL: Animal Ecology. *Illus.* TB/543

W. H. DOWDESWELL: The Mechanism of Evolution. *Illus.* TB/527

R. W. GERARD: Unresting Cells. *Illus.* TB/541

DAVID LACK: Darwin's Finches. *Illus.* TB/544

J. E. MORTON: Molluscs: *An Introduction to their Form and Functions. Illus.* TB/529

O. W. RICHARDS: The Social Insects. *Illus.* TB/542

P. M. SHEPPARD: Natural Selection and Heredity. *Illus.* TB/528

EDMUND W. SINNOTT: Cell and Psyche: *The Biology of Purpose* TB/546

C. H. WADDINGTON: How Animals Develop. *Illus.* TB/553

Chemistry

J. R. PARTINGTON: A Short History of Chemistry. *Illus.* TB/522

J. READ: A Direct Entry to Organic Chemistry. *Illus.* TB/523

J. READ: Through Alchemy to Chemistry. *Illus.* TB/561

Geography

R. E. COKER: This Great and Wide Sea: *An Introduction to Oceanography and Marine Biology. Illus.* TB/551

F. K. HARE: The Restless Atmosphere TB/560

History of Science

W. DAMPIER, Ed.: Readings in the Literature of Science. *Illus.* TB/512

ALEXANDRE KOYRÉ: From the Closed World to the Infinite Universe: *Copernicus, Kepler, Galileo, Newton, etc.* TB/31

A. G. VAN MELSEN: From Atomos to Atom: *A History of the Concept* Atom TB/517

O. NEUGEBAUER: The Exact Sciences in Antiquity TB/552

H. T. PLEDGE: Science Since 1500: *A Short History of Mathematics, Physics, Chemistry and Biology. Illus.* TB/506

GEORGE SARTON: Ancient Science and Modern Civilization TB/501

HANS THIRRING: Energy for Man: *From Windmills to Nuclear Power* TB/556

WILLIAM LAW WHYTE: Essay on Atomism: *From Democritus to 1960* TB/565

A. WOLF: A History of Science, Technology and Philosophy in the 16th and 17th Centuries.° *Illus.*
Volume I TB/508
Volume II TB/509

A. WOLF: A History of Science, Technology, and Philosophy in the Eighteenth Century.° *Illus.*
Volume I TB/539
Volume II TB/540

Mathematics

H. DAVENPORT: The Higher Arithmetic: *An Introduction to the Theory of Numbers* TB/526

H. G. FORDER: Geometry: *An Introduction* TB/548

GOTTLOB FREGE: The Foundations of Arithmetic: *A Logico-Mathematical Enquiry into the Concept of Number* TB/534

S. KÖRNER: The Philosophy of Mathematics: *An Introduction* TB/547

D. E. LITTLEWOOD: Skeleton Key of Mathematics: *A Simple Account of Complex Algebraic Problems* TB/525

GEORGE E. OWEN: Fundamentals of Scientific Mathematics TB/569

WILLARD VAN ORMAN QUINE: Mathematical Logic TB/558

O. G. SUTTON: Mathematics in Action.° *Foreword by James R. Newman. Illus.* TB/518

FREDERICK WAISMANN: Introduction to Mathematical Thinking. *Foreword by Karl Menger* TB/511

Philosophy of Science

R. B. BRAITHWAITE: Scientific Explanation TB/515

J. BRONOWSKI: Science and Human Values. *Illus.* TB/505

ALBERT EINSTEIN: Philosopher-Scientist. *Edited by Paul A. Schilpp*
Volume I TB/502
Volume II TB/503

WERNER HEISENBERG: Physics and Philosophy: *The Revolution in Modern Science. Introduction by F. S. C. Northrop* TB/549

JOHN MAYNARD KEYNES: A Treatise on Probability.° *Introduction by N. R. Hanson* TB/557

STEPHEN TOULMIN: Foresight and Understanding: *An Enquiry into the Aims of Science. Foreword by Jacques Barzun* TB/564

STEPHEN TOULMIN: The Philosophy of Science: *An Introduction* TB/513

G. J. WHITROW: The Natural Philosophy of Time° TB/563

Physics and Cosmology

DAVID BOHM: Causality and Chance in Modern Physics. *Foreword by Louis de Broglie* TB/536

P. W. BRIDGMAN: The Nature of Thermodynamics TB/537

A. C. CROMBIE, Ed.: Turning Point in Physics TB/535

C. V. DURELL: Readable Relativity. *Foreword by Freeman J. Dyson* TB/530

ARTHUR EDDINGTON: Space, Time and Gravitation: *An outline of the General Relativity Theory* TB/510

GEORGE GAMOW: Biography of Physics Σ TB/567

MAX JAMMER: Concepts of Force: *A Study in the Foundation of Dynamics* TB/550

MAX JAMMER: Concepts of Mass *in Classical and Modern Physics* TB/571

MAX JAMMER: Concepts of Space: *The History of Theories of Space in Physics. Foreword by Albert Einstein* TB/533

EDMUND WHITTAKER: History of the Theories of Aether and Electricity
Volume I: *The Classical Theories* TB/531
Volume II: *The Modern Theories* TB/532

G. J. WHITROW: The Structure and Evolution of the Universe: *An Introduction to Cosmology. Illus.* TB/504

Code to Torchbook Libraries:

TB/1+ : The Cloister Library
TB/501+ : The Science Library
TB/1001+ : The Academy Library
TB/2001+ : The Bollingen Library
TB/3001+ : The University Library

A LETTER TO THE READER

Overseas, there is considerable belief that we are a country of extreme conservatism and that we cannot accommodate to social change.

Books about America in the hands of readers abroad can help change those ideas.

The U. S. Information Agency cannot, by itself, meet the vast need for books about the United States.

You can help.

Harper Torchbooks provides three packets of books on American history, economics, sociology, literature and politics to help meet the need.

To send a packet of Torchbooks [*] overseas, all you need do is send your check for $7 (which includes cost of shipping) to Harper & Row. The U. S. Information Agency will distribute the books to libraries, schools, and other centers all over the world.

I ask every American to support this program, part of a worldwide BOOKS USA campaign.

I ask you to share in the opportunity to help tell others about America.

EDWARD R. MURROW
Director,
U. S. Information Agency

[*retailing at $10.85 to $12.00]